Just Say Yes!

By

Michael Lourey

Promise Publishing Company
Orange, California 92668

Cover Design by Eric Booth
Edited by M.B. Steele

JUST SAY YES!
©1989 by Promise Publishing, Inc.
Published by Promise Publishing, Inc.
Orange, California 92668

Printed in the United States of America

Library of Congress
Cataloging-in-Publication Data

Lourey, Michael
    JUST SAY YES!

ISBN 0-939497-17-4

TABLE OF CONTENTS

INTRODUCTION

We have discovered that one of the greatest thrills in life is helping someone else to find the joy and freedom we have found in Christ! (Ezekiel 33:9-10 and Psalm 107:2, 8, 15, 21 & 31).

We know that experiencing temptation is not a sin. It becomes a sin when we respond to it in the wrong way. We found that we can learn how to deal with it in steps six, seven and eight (I Peter 1:7, Hebrews 4:15 and James 4:7).

We have determined to give what we should and to discover where and when to give. We have been takers long enough, we will now become givers! (I Corinthians 16:2).

We have begun our search for the will of God for our lives; how we can spend our lives to benefit His Kingdom. In our service to the Master, it is our availability, not our ability that counts! (II Peter 1:10).

EPILOGUE

JUST SAY YES!

DEDICATION

This work is dedicated to all those precious souls who were instrumental in helping us to discover the mechanics of this step by step, detailed pathway to finding freedom from the compulsions which grip each and every person on God's green earth. Although we know some will deny that they have any compulsions, we have come to discover that we are all flawed and in need of the deliverance of the Lord of Lords and the King of Kings.

We would also like to personally thank a few individuals who were intimately involved in the training leading up to the actual writing. Among the many people to whom we would like to publicly express our gratitude are Pastor John Rutherford, Pastor Verdon Henry, Pastor Dan Lindeman, Pastor Greg Austin and, of course, the most critical participant in this entire endeavor, the Holy Spirit of God! Special thanks to Pastor Dan Lindeman for his excellent addition to the work, the pages on water baptism. We would also like to dedicate this work to all people who have come to realize their need for deliverance and healing. We pray that through our effort in writing this, that they may find the answers and hope that they will need to sustain them in their journey through this pilgrim land.

Linda and I are certain that any who will commit their lives totally to the Lord will find the joy and peace He offers to be a reality, just as we have!

ACKNOWLEDGEMENT

In every venture as major as writing a book, there are a lot of "ups and downs," problems and unexpected challenges. Linda and I have had a friend who has experienced those emotions with us in the writing of this book. From the beginning, JoAnn Lockard was excited about having our book published and, even when we got tired or discouraged, she remained enthusiastic. Never once did we share our hearts with her without receiving words of understanding and encouragement. Not only this, but she has backed up her words with substantial gifts in support of our ministry.

Two other friends who have been irreplaceable in our lives are Pastor Tony Ponce and his wife, Diana. He has been in the ministry for ten years, the last three in Escondido where we met him. His compassionate heart and his experience in pastoring have made him a "spiritual father" to me. This cannot be artificially generated and I believe God has put him into my life for a "never-to-be-forgotten" role. My few words here cannot begin to express my gratitude for God's plan and for Tony's willingness to make himself available for its fulfillment.

Michael Lourey

THE PROBLEM

For I do not understand my own actions [I am baffled, bewildered]. I do not practice or accomplish what I wish, but I do the very thing that I loathe [which my moral instinct condemns]. For I know that nothing good dwells within me, that is in my flesh. I can will what is right, but I cannot perform it. [I have the intention and urge to do what is right, but no power to carry it out.] For I fail to practice the good deeds I desire to do, but the evil deeds that I do not desire to do are what I am [ever] doing. Now if I do what I do not desire to do, it is no longer I doing it [it is not myself that acts], but the sin [principle] which dwells within me [fixed and operating in my soul]. But I discern in my bodily members [in the sensitive appetites and wills of the flesh] a different law (rule of action) at war against the law of my mind (my reason) and making me a prisoner to the law of sin that dwells in my bodily organs [in the sensitive appetites and wills of the flesh]. O unhappy and pitiable and wretched man that I am! Who will release and deliver me from [the shackles of] this body of death? (Romans 8:15, 18, 19, 20, 23, 24)

THE SOLUTION

Let the redeemed of the Lord say so, who he has delivered from the hand of the adversary, some wandered in the wilderness in a solitary desert track; they found no city for habitation. Hungry and thirsty, they fainted; their lives were near to being extinguished. Some sat in darkness and in the shadow of death, being bound in affliction and in irons, because they had rebelled against the words of God and spurned the counsel of the Most High. Therefore, he bowed down their hearts with hard labor; they stumbled and fell down, and there was none to help. Some are fools [made ill] because of the way of their transgressions and are afflicted because of their iniquities, they loathe every kind of food, and they draw near to the gates of death. Then they cry to the Lord in their trouble and He delivers them out of their distresses. He sends forth His Word and heals them and rescues them from the pit and destruction. Oh, that men would praise (and confess to) the Lord for His goodness and loving-kindness and His wonderful works to the children of men! And let them sacrifice the sacrifices of thanksgiving and rehearse His deeds with shouts of joy and singing! (Psalm 107:2, 4-5, 10-12, 17-22)

INTRODUCTION

WHY DO WE NEED ANOTHER BOOK?

Many of us have heard about the three basic types of people; if you haven't, let me take this opportunity to fill you in. There are those who make it happen, those who watch it happen, and those who wonder what happened. We all know that it's not exactly that simple, but there is something which seems to cut across all different classes, races, types, education levels, financial levels, and what-have-you.

Somehow or other, we find that some people are victims of compulsive behavior patterns. Maybe it is alcohol, dope, eating, soft drinks, swearing, worrying, lying, or you-name-it, but the fact is that these problems are very hard to overcome. If we desire to change more than the outside evidence of the problem, we must look beyond our own sphere of power.

First, we must realize we have a basic problem, which is our sin nature. If we would overcome that problem, then we must have the help of a power greater than the power of sin. This leads us to a single and inescapable solution. This solution will be discovered in the pages of the inspired *Word of God*, the Bible.

Many people in both my experience and most probably in yours, have overcome the abusive habits on an external level with such things as psychology, AA, NA, etc. However, they have a constant battle for the rest of their lives. If you want to find an answer to this problem, this book may be for you!

The reason that I say that this book may be for you is that it will take a humble and honest admission of your own inadequacy and a genuine response to the urging of the Spirit of the *Living God* to begin the "New Life in Christ." Another item you will need is an ample amount of courage; many will mock and scorn you and many more will gainsay you in your effort to live your new life in the *Kingdom of God*. However, the Bible promises all the courage needed to those who will believe in Jesus Christ as their Lord and Savior. If you can admit your own inadequacy and if you have the necessary courage, plus a sincere desire to be once and for all forgiven and changed, read on.

If I haven't scared you off by now, let me give you a little encouragement at this time. For seventeen years, I suffered from a whole list of compulsive behavior disorders. The list is too lengthy to go through here, so let me assure you that the disorders on my list had destroyed and crippled all phases of my life. However, a servant of the *King of Kings and the Lord of Lords*, by the name of John Rutherford, who started a fellowship called New Life, took me through these steps and now I can truly say without a doubt, "I am a child of the Living God, set free by the blood of Jesus. He has broken every chain and every bondage of sin within my heart and life, and I'm a new creature in Christ Jesus. Old things are passed away, behold all things are become new and I'm seated together with Christ in the heavenly places, washed by the blood of the Lamb; my name is written in the Lamb's book of life; I'm changed by the power of the Almighty God!"

Is this for you? Only you can know; if the Spirit of God is tugging at your heart, take the first step toward your *New Life*.

HOW WILL THIS BOOK BE DIFFERENT?

Over the last few years, I have been involved in setting up and directing programs to teach people how to overcome drug and alcohol abuse. In almost every case, the material available to use has been of the sort which tries to keep the Creator in a very small box. I suppose that my religious training and my simplistic view of scriptures tend to make me uncomfortable with this approach to a person's life. I firmly believe that our God, through the blood of Jesus, by the power of the Holy Spirit not only can, but will change our lives. If He cannot, then the Bible is a lie and I for one cannot accept that.

There is no doubt that the experience that I had (when I was in desperation and I reached out to find the only true hope) has affected my concept. You see, I didn't leave that altar partially changed, almost new, or any other foolishness. When I prayed to the Lord to receive forgiveness for my sins and for

3

Jesus to step in and rule my life, God did exactly what He said He would do. The old Michael died there and a new creature in place and time got up and walked away with his Lord and Savior as a constant companion. The indwelling of the Spirit of God was a reality and I was indeed a new man.

Of course, many have questioned this experience, but I have seen it repeated in too many others both before and since it happened to me to question it myself. I believe that we either admit that the entire Bible is the truth and is without error or, we must logically believe that it is entirely a work of fiction. Whichever view you have will determine whether or not you will be interested in beginning this book. If you choose to try to straddle the fence and not believe one way or the other, don't bother even wasting a minute more of your time. That type of commitment will not enable you to gain anything from a book which not only deals with absolutes, but strongly encourages belief in them as the only road to survival.

Just let me caution you though; a stance which makes no decision is simply a decision to say, "No," without the guts to say it! In this book, we will not be attempting to teach you how to turn over a new leaf, but rather to teach you how to receive and to live in the joyous reality of a *NEW LIFE IN CHRIST*. We also will not be teaching you techniques for an ongoing battle with whatever compulsive behavior problems you have. If you can grasp the teaching in this book, and through prayer make them a reality in your life, you will not battle with those problems anymore. Be warned however, this is not an offer of a panacea, which will forever end all of your current or future problems. What we will offer is the assurance that you will never battle problems without the Savior and that no temptation will overtake you without the Savior providing a way of escape.

Again, let me encourage you to find out if something like this could be for you; after all, the only way you will know for sure is by personal experience.

WHO WROTE THIS BOOK?

At this time, let me take a few lines to tell you a little about myself and about why this book was written. I am not a Bible scholar and don't have a degree in theology; I simply serve the Lord as He directs and trust the consequences to Him. Before I met the *Living Lord*, my life was characterized by frustration, sickness, crime, hopelessness, degradation, addictions and hatred. The moment I met Jesus, all this changed and now my life is His to do with as He pleases.

Being one who always enjoyed fighting and strife, I found in the service of the Lord all the battles I could ever want. As Christians we have three basic enemies:

1. Satan,

2. The world, and

3. Our old sin nature.

These three keep me busy enough that I don't have to look elsewhere for a fight. The *Good News* is that Jesus is with me every step of the way and as long as I am being submissive and obedient to Him, the victory is always His.

This book is being written at the urging of the Holy Spirit as He gives me utterance and it is my sincere desire that His love will be transmitted through these pages as strongly as I am experiencing it as I write. My desire is to write down the things the Holy Spirit tells me to write. In my association with "New Life Ministries," I have seen a multitude of people who have, by the sacrifice made at Calvary, had their lives changed in miraculous fashion. The *Hand of God* has been so much in evidence that all attempts to explain away the wonder working power of the Holy Spirit fall in the dust of empty philosophy. Alcoholics are no longer alcoholics; addicts are set free; homosexuals are delivered; all manner of sin-filled lifestyles are transformed by Him.

Could something like this be for you? These miracles are not something that can be earned or deserved; they are a free gift of God and as the Bible says, *"Whosoever will, let him take the water of life freely."*

Pastor John Rutherford (I mentioned him earlier) gave my wife and me a prayer years ago. This prayer has had a profound effect on our walk with the Lord and upon our lives here in this world. We would like to share it with you at this time. It has been a blessing at times of need and a comfort in times of plenty. We hope that it will minister to you as well!

Jesus,
I give up all my own desires and hopes,
and accept Your will for my life.
I give myself, my life,
my all utterly to You to be Yours forever.
Fill me and seal me with Your Holy Spirit.
Use me as You will,
cause me to serve You where I am
or move me where You will.
Work out Your whole will in my life at any cost,
now and forever.
Amen.

HOW DO I USE THIS BOOK?

The only other book you will need is a Bible. Find a translation which you can understand and use it as long as you feel comfortable with it. All scriptural references included in this book are from the Amplified Version, to aid your comprehension. Should you find a verse in the Bible you use which you don't understand, you may want to consult another version for clarification.

If I've never read the Bible, will I be able to use this book?

That will make little or no difference; in fact if you have never read or studied it, you may have an easier time comprehending the material since you will have no preconceived notions. The Books of the

Bible will be listed in its table of contents. Finding chapter and verse is easy to learn.

What if I already have a religion or none at all?

Since we will be using both Old and New Testaments as our resources for learning about God, your religion at the outset is not important. We only encourage you to approach it with an open mind and a willingness to be set free from your compulsions. Even if you doubt God, or His existence, you will still benefit from this book experientially.

How will implementing this book bring about changes in my life?

As it says in Isaiah 55:11,

> *So shall My Word be that goes forth out of My mouth: It shall not return to Me void [without production, any effect, useless], but it shall accomplish that which I please and purpose and it shall prosper in the thing for which I sent it.*

We believe this to be the absolute truth, therefore it will have an effect on your life.

Would it help to study this book with others?

Meeting regularly with others who are also using this book will be of great value to your progress. We do suggest, however, that in your group there should be a person who is not dealing with compulsive behavior problems. It would be best if this person is one who has experienced God's miraculous healing power and is a mature Christian. This time of sharing and working together should enhance your understanding of God and His character. The acceptance, encouragement, and support of others will also help you to be ready to accept and experience God's healing for your life!

1. In choosing your Bible, avoid Bibles which are used in cult religions; these will not lead you to an understanding which will be beneficial to your healing and deliverance, or to your eternal life.

2. If you have a mature Christian to help you, the following tools will be helpful for him or her: Berry's Expository Dictionary, Strong's Concordance and Vine's Interlinear Greek/English New Testament.

WHAT ARE OUR RESOURCES?

You will find as you read, that the Bible is chuck full of good advice. But then, so are a few other good books. The problem is that we will almost always resist good advice. God's promises are also written out for us in the Bible, the good gifts He wants to give us, the healing power of His Spirit, and His precious love which He wants to freely give us. However, if all we see in the scriptures is a load of good advice and an abundance of promises, the Bible is no better than any of the self help or positive thinking pulp works which abound today.

Praise God, the Bible has more to it than a bunch of promises and advice. The Bible is our guide book to God's power and grace. It is our only true source of freedom. The Bible is not a "self help book," but rather a "God help book" which directs us to *His power* and teaches us to live in *His promises* and to attain *His Kingdom.*

In the Bible, we will find a number of covenants; however, we will be dwelling on the covenant which Christ made for us on the Cross of Calvary. He has once and for all defeated the power and penalty of sin for all those who will turn to God with a repentant heart, turning by faith toward Jesus, believing that He died and was resurrected to eternal life. Indeed, if Jesus has residence in your heart, evil has no place there.

The healing and deliverance we need are always very near to us and, at the same time, separated by a great gulf. This gulf may only be bridged from God's side. With Jesus Christ as our Lord and Savior, we are made children of God and joint heirs with Christ, in His kingdom. This adoption into the family of God, enables us to have our unhappy and unproductive lives transformed into lives which are characterized by joyfulness and productivity.

To begin receiving these promises, and to have the scriptural guidelines become a reality in our lives, we need to have that gulf bridged. The purpose of this book is to show us in God's Word, the Bible, how He will accomplish this in our lives. God wants us to come home to Him. He desires that none should perish. We were, after all, created to fellowship with Him. If we are caught up in the snares and traps of the Devil, we are precluded from that fellowship. However, if we will turn from our wickedness toward His righteousness, He will welcome us like the father welcomed the prodigal son in Luke 15.

But still we ask, how will all of this cause God to help me stop doing the things which are destroying me? Theologians have just as hard a time with that question as do non-believers. In seeking the answer, we will use these twelve steps and the Bible, which is the inspired Word of God. We believe that by the time you have finished step twelve, you will find that the question doesn't matter anymore as the problem will be gone!

How can I know that the Bible will be my resource for freeing me of my compulsions?

THE BIBLE ITSELF PROMISES TO BE OUR GUIDE!

Psalm 119:130 -

The entrance and unfolding of Your words give light; their unfolding gives understanding (discernment and comprehension) to the simple.

II Peter 1:19 -

And we have the prophetic word [made] firmer still. You will do well to pay close attention to it as to a lamp shining in a dismal (squalid and dark) place, until the day breaks through [the gloom] and the Morning Star rises (comes into being) in your hearts.

Psalm 119:9 -

How shall a young man cleanse his way? By taking heed and keeping watch [on himself] according to Your word [conforming his life to it].

John 17:17 -

Sanctify them [purify, consecrate, separate them for yourself, make them holy] by Truth; Your Word is Truth.

Romans 15:4 -

For whatever was thus written in former days was written for our instruction, that by [our steadfast and patient] endurance and the encouragement [drawn] from the Scriptures we might hold fast to and cherish hope.

Romans 8:2 -

For the law of the Spirit of life [which is] in Christ Jesus [the law of our new being] has freed me from the law of sin and of death.

WHAT IS YOUR PERSONAL RESPONSE?

_____
_____
_____
_____
_____
_____
_____
_____
_____
_____

STEP ONE

For seventeen years drugs ruled my life; for the last twelve years of that seventeen, alcohol became a co-ruler. Considering the amounts and frequency of my substance abuse, the term "social user" wouldn't have been even close to the truth, although I maintained that I was in control and could quit any time that I wanted. I had come to believe that drugs and alcohol were the only means I had of making myself feel that I belonged or fit in.

Although I had experimented with some drugs prior to late 1966, the heavy use didn't start until I was in Korea with the army. I was assigned to the Second Infantry Division and was stationed at Camp Reddick. Camp Reddick was above the Injin River and it was the home base of Company C, 1st Battalion, 38th Infantry.

We pulled all of our duty patrolling the DMZ both in daytime hunter/killer patrols and nighttime ambush missions. The two bizarre elements of this duty were:

1. We couldn't fire on the enemy without permission, even if we were under attack; and

2. We were to be an expendable delaying force in the event that the North Koreans decided to reopen hostilities.

There were only two bridges across the Injin River in the UN Sector, Freedom Bridge and Libby Bridge. Camp Reddick was about ten miles above Libby Bridge and it would be blown if a North Korean incursion occurred. Obviously we felt a certain amount of pressure under these circumstances. To further complicate matters we were engaged in fighting a war that supposedly had ended in the Fifties.

During my thirteen month stay in Korea, some friends and I discovered how easy it was to get opium and pot. Since none of us liked to drink, these seemed the perfect way to forget the tension of our daily lives. As is usually the case, we started depending on these artificial means to get us through more than our free time. As soon as we were given some "cross tops," we discovered that we could get mellow with the pot, get lost in the opium and get straight with the cross tops. This way we didn't have to deal with a reality that was beyond our comprehension.

Since the only place to socialize in Korea was in the bars, I eventually gave in to the peer pressure to begin to drink. Without even realizing it, I had chosen to add alcohol to the growing problem of drug abuse in my life. By the time I left Korea in January, 1967, daily drug and alcohol use had become an integral part of my ability to have fun, and to cope with my circumstances. At this point I didn't perceive it as a problem for I thought I was still in control and could quit any time I wanted to. The danger signals were there, I just failed to see them. After all, we knew reality was for people who couldn't handle drugs.

After a short stint at Fort Lewis, Washington as a drill sergeant, I was sent to Viet Nam. Here I was again in a foreign land with a new twist. While I was at Fort Lewis, it was discovered that I had had a seizure disorder since I was thirteen years old. With that history, the Army (in all of it's insight) decided that I could no longer be trusted with a weapon. Somehow, that didn't seem to matter to the Army since in December of 1968, I found myself in South Viet Nam. Now I was not only in a combat zone, but I was unarmed!

Needless to say, I wasn't very happy with my circumstances and decided that the only way to cope was to stay "blown away." I soon discovered that pot and opium weren't going to do the trick anymore. Someone turned me on to a mixture of heroin and cocaine. We called them speed balls; just what I needed. Now I could walk around and not care about anything. In a short period of time, I wound up in a hospital in Camp Zama, Japan, in the neuropsychiatric ward. It seemed that they thought I was nuts just because I told an officer I was going to kill him. One day, we were out in the field building a floating bridge and we drew some sniper fire. This made me a little nervous so I asked the officer in charge what I was supposed to do if we came under a heavy attack. He said, "Fight," and I said, "How? You won't let me have a gun."

He said, "Well then, I suppose you will just have to die, you lousy freak..." Actually, I handled the whole thing fairly calmly. All I did was explain to him that he had better pray that I would be the first to die, because if anyone dropped their weapon, he would be the first one I'd kill.

Shortly, I was in the hospital at Camp Zama. All the patients in my ward were compelled to take drugs which were designed to keep us really mellow. Some of the drugs were thorazine and chloral-hydrate. If we chose not to take them, we would be locked up by ourselves in a little room with nothing but a hole in the floor. If we still refused, they would restrain us and inject us. For someone who liked drugs this may have sounded ideal but the problem was that the thorazine caused me to have seizures.

When I finally got to talk to a doctor and to explain this to him, his first response was to call me a malingerer. After I insisted that I was telling the truth, in a very loud manner, he decided to see for himself. What he did was to strap me in a chair, hook me up to an EEG and inject me with a massive dose of thorazine. After I went into convulsions, he believed me. He sent me to a holding company until I could be returned to the States.

It seemed that everywhere the Army sent me turned out to offer more opportunities to experiment and abuse drugs. Somewhere in the midst of all this, my ability to control the drugs turned into their ability to control me.

Along with the increased use and abuse came quite a few personality changes. Anger and frustration coupled with self-hate and violence became a way of life. Not long after my discharge from the Army, I got involved with an outlaw motorcycle club, eventually becoming an officer in one of their chapters. It seemed that everything I did and everywhere I went only brought more opportunity to get loaded and less control over the situations of my life.

Just prior to my time with the motorcycle club, Linda and I met and were married. At the time, she didn't know of my destructive habits, since we met during one of my periods of being clean. For the next ten years, she devoted herself to changing me and the habitual behavior I demonstrated. Since Linda was a CPA and I could always get jobs in sales or start businesses which would be successful for a while, we always made an abundance of money. But whatever I didn't spend on drinking and using, she spent on trying to get me well. Consequently, we always ran out of money before we ran out of month.

Finally in 1980, we decided to buy a bar and restaurant. Our reasoning seemed sound at the time. We figured that since I spent seventeen or eighteen hours a day in bars, we should buy one and keep the money in the family. Within about three months from the time we took over the bar, it was making about $10,000.00 a month. By this time I had given up on the idea of ever changing and had resigned myself to dying young. During the years between 1972 and 1980 Linda had spent everything she could on every treatment method we came across. We tried everything from AA to psychiatric inpatient programs. We had even tried the "positive thinking" programs and mystic religions. Nothing seemed to offer any permanent help. I would clean up for a short period of time, but the same old habits and happenings would reappear and I would revert right back to what I had always been, "a square peg in a round hole."

By the end of 1981, we were bankrupt and contemplating divorce. During the previous year, I had spent over $350,000 on my habits and Linda was ready to give up, too. We decided to give it one last chance and moved to California, only to find the same people with different names and faces waiting for us.

By mid-1983, I was in the psychiatric ward of the Long Beach VA Hospital. Finally, I was faced with my own failure and death was ready for me, but I was not ready for it!

STEP ONE
ADMIT YOUR LACK OF SELF CONTROL

We admitted that we were out of control and that our compulsion was ruling our lives - our lives had become unmanageable.

The first problem we had to face was to identify and name the thing that had taken control of us and our lives. The world with all of its scholars and experts, can give us names and identities for what they feel the problem is. However, they don't realize that they are naming a symptom rather than a problem.

You see, terms like alcoholic, drug addict, homosexual, etc., are merely symptoms of a much deeper problem. The root of this behavior is found in the third chapter of the first book of the Bible. What we have in psychiatry is a group of people who think they have all the answers when they don't even know the question (1 Timothy 6:20). Worldly wisdom will tell you that your compulsive behavior is a disease. This is nothing more than a transparent deception which is aimed at causing you to believe that you are always going to be "sick." In doing this, the health care community believes that they can keep you dependent on them and their system.

Don't be confused by this deception. The Almighty God has the power and the will to forever change your life, if you will only believe. Although your compulsion is not in itself a physical problem, it will manifest itself in any number of physical problems. When the root problem has been eradicated, the physical symptoms usually leave, too. The associated problems of guilt, anxiety, fear and negative feelings will also be dealt with by the curing of the basic problem. By now you should be wondering what the "root problem" is. If you haven't already figured it out, it is our sin nature.

The unforgiven sin in our lives can lead to compulsive behavior and separate us from God. When we are in bondage to something of this world we cannot, at the same time, serve God. Lust, is what leads us to compulsive behavior, and according to James 1:13-18,

> *Let no one say when he is tempted, I am tempted from God; for God is incapable of being tempted by [what is] evil and He Himself tempts no one. But every person is tempted when he is drawn away, enticed and baited by his own evil desire (lust, passions). Then the evil desire, when it has conceived, gives birth to sin, and sin, when it is fully matured, brings forth death. Do not be misled, my beloved brethren. Every good gift and every perfect (free, large, full) gift is from above; It comes down from the Father of all [that gives] light, in [the shining of] whom there can be no variation [rising or setting] or shadow cast by His turning [as in an eclipse]. And it was of His own [free] will that He gave us birth [as sons] by [His] word of truth, so that we should be a kind of first-fruits of His creatures [a sample of what He created to be consecrated to Himself].*

We say in Step One, that our lives have become unmanageable as a result of our lust and it cripples our mind, body and spirit. It also has a very damaging effect on all external areas of our lives. Because of these damaging effects our compulsion is both life-threatening and life-confusing. In Step One, we also admit our powerlessness in dealing with our compulsion.

Even though you may be ready to admit that you are powerless, you probably don't realize just how powerless you really are and just how unmanageable your life has become. Our compulsions cloud our thinking and, therefore, we are mostly unaware of how damaging our behavior is to ourselves and those around us. Most often the compulsive behavior problems have progressed in such a gradual manner that we are basically unaware of the extent of our loss of ability to function. Think about it! What alcoholic started out with his or her first drink thinking and looking forward to the day he would be alcoholic? In fact, if we look at our situation in the light of truth, we will find that the things, which are now compulsive problems, started out as something we did for pleasure or gratification. At one time, we doubtlessly felt that it not only helped us, but that it was our answer for things we wouldn't or couldn't deal with. You may feel that, for the most part, you are still making good choices. What we don't notice, however, is that we are continually making the same choice - to do or to have more of what is killing us.

Take Step One now, don't wait until you have cleaned up your life because that day will never come! You may have discovered that when you began to realize that your life was out of control, a sense of depression began to make the very things that had been giving you pleasure or gratification, cause you to feel even worse. Maybe you can still go from feeling bad to feeling a little better if you can just get enough, you may think. But by now the progression should be obvious. The things which once "worked" for you are now turning on you and you realize that either you will reach a point where you can't get enough or else it will kill you outright. Only then can you acknowledge that you can no longer turn away from your compulsion on your own; you are powerless to make a change.

My friend, you are in a moment of decision, turn to Jesus now or live with your pain now and in Hell forever!

1. Why am I powerless?

Genesis 6:5 -

The Lord saw that the wickedness of man was great in the earth, and that every imagination and intention of all human thinking was only evil continually.

The entire fifty-first Psalm is one you should read all the way through but here is verse 5 -

Behold, I was brought forth in [a state of] iniquity; my mother was sinful who conceived me [and I too am sinful].

Isaiah 64:6 says -

For we have all become like one who is unclean [ceremonially, like a leper], and all our righteousness (our best deeds of rightness and justice) is like filthy rags or a polluted garment; we all fade like a leaf, and our iniquities, like the wind, take us away [far from God's favor, hurrying us toward destruction].

WHAT IS YOUR PERSONAL RESPONSE?

_____

_____

_____

_____

_____

_____

From the first book of the Bible through the last, we find man's condition unchanged. Despite all of the miracles and deliverances God performs, despite all the love He gives, despite all the compassion He displays, mankind continually gives back sin and iniquity.[1]

When Adam and Eve first sinned, they sold our righteousness for a piece of fruit. Since then, Satan has been the ruler of this world. Our thoughts and aims invariably turn out wrong and we seem powerless to alter our basic nature. Due to our sin nature, we are born in sin and continue in it all of our days.

The original language of the Old Testament graphically describes what is comparable to our righteousness. On top of that, our sins will take us on a path of sure destruction and ruin, in this life and for eternity. On our own, we are hopeless and helpless.

Can you still ask, "Why do I need Jesus?" Of course, you are free to go the route of the world today and decide that your own willpower and intelligence will be the answer. Remember though, it was your intelligence that got you into the mess you are in now. As for your willpower, I'd venture to say that you have lots of willpower, the problem is that you don't have any won't power!

2.   Can't this problem be solved by will power and intelligent thought?

Proverbs 3:5 -

Lean on, trust in, and be confident in the Lord with all your and mind and do not rely on your own insight or under-standing.

Romans 7:18 -

For I know that nothing good dwells within me, that is, in my flesh. I can will what is right, but I cannot perform it. [I have the intention and urge to do what is right, but no power to carry it out].

Philippians 4:13 -

I have strength for all things in Christ Who empowers me [I am ready for anything and equal to anything through Him Who infuses inner strength into me; I am self-sufficient in Christ's sufficiency].

Philippians 4:19 -

And my God will liberally supply (fill to the full) your every need according to His riches in glory in Christ Jesus.

WHAT IS YOUR PERSONAL RESPONSE?

_____

_____

_____

_____

_____

_____

God's Word has just told us who to trust and who not to trust. Why is our decision so difficult? Because we have been taught a pack of lies all of our lives. It is not weakness that causes us to admit our lack of power or self control. It takes courage to take a step of faith, to believe in Someone with the power and authority to cause genuine change.[3]

Even if we have the will to change, the ability to accomplish this miracle will be lacking.[4]

I'm not saying that without God man has never done any good; I'm saying that the only sustained eternal good is from God. Are you afraid of what people will think? I hate to pop your balloon. They already think worse of you than you can imagine. In Philippians, we are told of the source of power who gives us the ability to do good and to change our lives for the better on a permanent basis. When we come home to the family of God, through Jesus Christ, we become joint heirs of the entire universe and everything in it. Whatever our needs are, we can be assured that they will be supplied.[5]

This shouldn't be confused with our greed, want, lust, or any other foolish desire. Don't be deceived by false teachers who would have you believe that God has nothing better to do than wait for you to express your will so He can perform it. Don't be deceived, God is not a genie waiting inside a magic lamp.

Of course, if you haven't suffered enough yet at the hands of this world, you can trust your life and your eternity to learned experts, (by the way, an expert is someone who knows more and more, about less and less until he knows absolutely everything, about absolutely nothing). The problem you will encounter is that to them you are a paycheck; to God you are a lost child. Who will care more?

3. Doesn't psychology or psychiatry have the answers? How about things like "ESP" or some of the mystic religions?

Ecclesiastes 1:18 -

For in much [human] wisdom is much vexation, and he who increases knowledge increases sorrow.

Colossians 2:8 -

See to it that no one carries you off as spoil or makes you yourselves captive by his so-called philosophy and intellectualism and vain deceit (idle fancies and plain nonsense), following human tradition (men's ideas of the material rather than the spiritual world), just crude notions following the rudimentary and elemental teachings of the universe and disregarding [the teachings of] Christ (the Messiah).

I Timothy 6:20 -

Timothy, guard and keep the deposit entrusted [to you]! Turn away from the irreverent babble and godless chatter, with the vain and empty and worldly phrases, and the subtleties and the contradictions in what is falsely called knowledge and spiritual illumination.

WHAT IS YOUR PERSONAL RESPONSE?

_____

_____

_____

_____

_____

_____

Solomon, the son of David who became the wealthiest and most successful ruler whom the world has ever seen, wrote the words of the first scripture we just quoted. He is known in history as the wisest man who ever lived and yet, he writes that a lot of wisdom and learning bring increased sorrow. He is speaking here about wisdom under the sun, not wisdom above the sun (that is, from God).

Today, we have the opportunity of listening to and learning from people who are no happier or more prepared for eternity than we are. They can teach us philosophy and man's learning, but they cannot give us answers, only questions. By now, you probably have enough questions. Some think that science has all the answers, but what they don't know is, all true science is biblically based. Again and again it is proven that the only lasting truths are to be found in the Bible.

Did you know that there is more historical and archeological proof that the Bible is true than there is that George Washington ever lived? Where do you want to put your trust, in an unprovable theory or in the proven, factual Word of God? It's your eternity that's on the line; don't make any more foolish decisions based on incomplete or incorrect information. Jesus died for you; that is the truth![6]

4. How can I know that I am powerless to get well on my own?

Ecclesiastes 2:26 -

For to the person who pleases Him God gives wisdom and knowledge and joy; but to the sinner He gives the work of gathering and heaping up, that he may give to one who pleases God. This also is vanity and a striving after the wind and a feeding on it.

John 3:27 -

John answered, A man can receive nothing [he can claim nothing, he can take unto himself nothing] except as it has been granted to him from heaven. [A man must be content to receive the gift which is given him from heaven; there is no other source].

II Corinthians 3:5 -

Not that we are fit (qualified and sufficient in ability) of ourselves to form personal judgments or to claim or count anything as coming from us, but our power and ability and sufficiency are from God.

I Peter 2:24 -

He personally bore our sins in His [own] body on the tree [as on an altar and offered Himself on it], that we might die (cease to exist) to sin and live to righteousness. By His wounds you have been healed.

WHAT IS YOUR PERSONAL RESPONSE?

_____

_____

_____

_____

_____

_____

The fact that you are where you are now, without hope and power, should tell you that within you there is no power to change. Join us at the cross of Jesus Christ and find true peace and freedom. Do it now; you can be permanently free!

In Matthew 17:17, we find the story of a man who came to Jesus to ask that his son be delivered and even the disciples couldn't help him. Jesus said,

...O you unbelieving (warped, wayward, rebellious) and thoroughly perverse generation! How long am I to remain with you? How long am I to bear with you? Bring him here to Me.

When Jesus rebuked the unclean spirit, the boy
was instantly cured. If (and it is true) God is the
same yesterday, today, and tomorrow,[7] can we expect anything less today? If we are in bondage to a
compulsion, we need the healing touch of the Savior
(also read Mark 9:17-27); only He is able to permanently break the bondage which has us in its
grip!

ADDITIONAL SCRIPTURES

1. Genesis 6:5 and Romans 3:10
2. Psalm 51
3. Romans 7:18
4. Romans 7:19
5. Philippians 4:19
6. I Corinthians 15:3
7. Hebrews 13:8b

STEP TWO

Before I graduated from high school, I had attended fifteen schools. Even in my earliest memories, it seemed that wherever my family lived, I just didn't fit in. My family was a fairly close one and our needs were always met, as my father was a hard worker. It just seemed that I was a step or two off the pace all the time. Loneliness dogged my every step and I became a loner, even when other people were around. Add to that the fact that accidents and disasters seemed to follow me and a picture of frustration begins to develop.

My grandparents didn't want me around because I made them too nervous. My friends' parents got tired of things breaking whenever I was around. I remember times when I could just walk through a room and things would fall off the walls or break. Fighting seemed to be a way to keep people at a distance, so I developed a very belligerent attitude on the outside. However, on the inside the pain and loneliness persisted and actually developed into strong feelings of inferiority. I knew something was terribly wrong, I just didn't know what it was or what to do about it.

As early as first grade, teachers were sending notes to my parents about having problems controlling me. When I was about twelve, a friend of my father's, who was an alcoholic and a wife beater, suddenly turned up, seemingly a new man. He had become a preacher. I guess that my parents thought that he might have a good influence on me so they sent me to his church every Sunday. I don't remember anything that happened there, but my Mother says that I was born again and spoke in tongues. For a period of about six to nine months, there was a change for the good. Then I received a severe head injury and all of the old problems came back, this time intensified. That period of time is a blank to me but my mother has told me what went on.

Over the following years, I tried many things to fill the loneliness I felt, including religions and psychiatric counselling in high school. By the time I was discharged from the Army (with a General Discharge for the "good of the service"), I felt, like Solomon, that everything under the sun was as useful as chasing the wind. Even when business ventures were successful or I landed a good job, the emptiness persisted. By the time I was twenty-three, I had been promoted to the position of regional sales trainer for Great Books of the Western World, yet still there was no relief. My first marriage was on the rocks and drugs had almost totally taken control. I felt that I could hide in them for a while, away from the world which was only pain and heartache to me.

In 1972, I met Linda, who is still my wife, and she undertook the task of making my life better. Linda was an advocate of "positive thinking" and as such she thought that every cloud had a silver lining, and I thought that every silver lining had a cloud. She thought that time heals all wounds and I thought time wounds all heels. Do you get the picture?

I did try positive thinking and wound up being positive that everything that could go wrong would, at the worst possible moment! During the next few years, Linda and I spent a tremendous amount of money trying to find answers. After many, many false hopes and empty failures, the thought of any more unsuccessful attempts at changing was almost unbearable. I had found an abundance of people who could tell me that I had problems (as if I didn't already know). The real problem was that they didn't have any answers that made any lasting difference.

Over the years, various people had been trying to tell me that the problem was a God-shaped vacuum inside my heart. I knew better than that though; my heart was only a muscle used to pump blood. Not only that, they seemed to be no less confused than I was and certainly no happier. Besides that, I had noticed that the way they acted around "Church People," and the way they acted around others was not the same; in fact, they appeared to be just as phony as everyone else. Therefore, I thought, "I, at least, am not a phony." Satan had really done a good job of deceiving me, as my focus was on the "created" and not the "Creator."

When Linda and I were on the verge of divorce (only a couple of months away from the final decree), an acquaintance of mine invited me to come and hear the presentation of a very large and successful multi-level business opportunity. When I saw the potential for success, I thought, "Maybe if we were rich, Linda and I could figure some way to be happy."

To make a long story short, we joined and became moderately successful very quickly. However, happiness still wasn't there and I was becoming disillusioned again. About then I noticed that some of the most successful people in this business were devoted Christians. It seemed that their faith was solid and they acted the same under all circumstances. They also had an inner peace, which I felt was the last hope for me.

One night, in a restaurant in La Palma, California, we were looking for some new people to sponsor in our business. We met a man and his wife who seemed genuinely interested in Linda and me. We followed up on these new prospects just as we had been taught and suddenly we found ourselves confronted with the invitation to go to church with them the following Sunday. When we couldn't find a good excuse, we reluctantly agreed to go. After all, we felt if we went to church with them, they would be obligated to listen to the opportunity we were offering. I knew that I was lacking something, and felt that they might know where to find it. As it turned out, what I was missing was God in my life.

During that service on Sunday, January 22, 1984, the Spirit of the Living God convicted me not only of needing Him, but of my life being all wrong and of my own lack of power to change it. The moment I heard the Gospel of Jesus Christ, my heart was no longer just "a muscle to pump blood." It was also an empty vessel which would not be content until it was no longer empty. At that moment I knew what I was missing and made the only decision that I (a person with lots of problems and no answers) could reasonably make when confronted with what I suddenly knew was the truth; I needed God!

STEP TWO
DISCOVER YOUR NEED FOR GOD

We discovered our need for Almighty God to restore sanity in our lives before it was too late. We no longer wanted to be separated from His presence.

In today's self-centered world, even to come to a realization of the Living God is a major revelation. Everything that we have been taught and all of our internal inclinations tell us that man is the center of the universe. If man is inherently good and he is the center of the universe, why is everything so out of control and why are we so hopeless?

Mankind has attempted to give us many false gods (actually the false gods come from the ruler of this world, Satan); we are encouraged to worship self, money, sex, positive thinking, cars, people, good works, religions and a long list of other equally worthless objects. In time, we become so lost that we don't even realize that we are lost. You know the feeling; something is wrong, something is missing

but I can't seem to put my finger on the problem. In
this state of confusion, we begin to cast about for
something or someone to believe in. Many times,
God is the last thing we are willing to try since we
have either been taught a false concept of Him or we
know nothing about Him at all.

Haven't you ever wondered, "If there is a God,
how can He let me hurt so?" or "If there is a God, why
doesn't He do something?" The problem we face, is
not that God will not, or cannot do anything, it is
that we haven't even realized that He is real and
that His promises are for us. No matter who you are
or where you have been, His promises are real. No
one gets preferential treatment in God's Kingdom.
Basically, the decision that we face is whether we
will make a choice to admit our need for God now
and no longer be separated from Him or wait until
death overtakes us and then admit His reality. The
problem with the latter course is that if you wait
until after you die to find out that He is real and you
cannot deny Him, then it is too late! Are you really
willing to gamble with an eternity of torment, just
for a few moments of foolish, unsatisfying, powerless, pride in self?

1. How can I know that I need God?

Genesis 3:6 & 7 -

*And when the woman saw that the tree was
good (suitable and pleasant) for food and that
it was delightful to look at, and a tree to be
desired in order to make one wise, she took of
its fruit and ate; and she gave some also to her*

husband, and he ate. Then the eyes of them both were opened, and they knew that they were naked; and they sewed fig leaves together and made themselves apronlike girdles.

Isaiah 59:2 & 3 -

But your iniquities have made a separation between you and your God, and your sins have hidden His face from you, so that He will not hear. For your hands are defiled with blood and your fingers with iniquity; your lips have spoken lies, your tongue mutters wickedness.

Luke 16:25 & 26 -

But Abraham said, "Child, remember that you in your lifetime fully received [what is due you in] comforts and delights, and Lazarus in like manner the discomforts and distresses; but now he is comforted here and you are in anguish. And besides all this, between us and you a great chasm has been fixed, in order that those who want to pass from this [place] to you may not be able, and no one may pass from there to us."

WHAT IS YOUR PERSONAL RESPONSE?

_____

_____

_____

_____

_____

The scriptures we have just written show us three separate types of sins. We see the original sin of Adam; from our perspective his sin doesn't seem all that big. All he did was take a bite of a piece of fruit. The problem is that God had commanded that Adam could eat of every tree in the garden except that one.[1]

If he (Adam) ate of that tree, God said that he would die. Until Adam ate that fruit, he was morally innocent. The moment he ate it, he became, by nature, a sinner. That is the death which God spoke of, the spiritual death.[2]

Since Adam is the federal head of the human family, we all became, by nature, sinners. Since apples beget apples and cows beget cows, it follows that since Adam sinned before the birth of his offspring, all mankind is therefore, by nature, sinful. Because of Adam's sin, death of the physical body, and death of the spirit entered into the world.[3]

By this we see what sin does. Sin, regardless of what sin it is, always causes separation. Sin separates us from God.[4] This separation from God is characterized by death. That mankind is sinful is proven by the fact that he dies. Where there is sin there is death.[5] (Romans 6:23a, " *For the wages which sin pays is death*"). The only remedy for this condition is life (union with God) (Romans 6:23b, *"But the [bountiful] free gift of God is eternal life through [in union with] Jesus Christ our Lord")*. Indeed, we will all die physically, but that death for the believer in Jesus

Christ, will only be the doorway into the presence of the Living God.[6]

We can also see the difference between repented sin and unrepented sin. Even though the rich man had it made while he was alive, in death his unrepented sins separated him from God. So you see, if we do not discover our need for God and take steps to secure the reality of His Son in our hearts and lives now, before it is too late, we will be like the rich man and face the impassable chasm.

Another important question arises at this point and it has to do with our worthiness to be helped. What have we done to deserve His unmerited favor, His grace? When we have taken a realistic inventory of our lives, that is a pretty scary question. As we will find out next, our "deservedness" has nothing to do with His willingness to move into our lives.[7]

2. How can I know that God will help me?

Isaiah 41:10 -

Fear not [there is nothing to fear], for I am with you; do not look around you in terror and be dismayed, for I am your God. I will strengthen and harden you to difficulties, yes, I will help you; yes, I will hold you up and retain you with My [victorious] right hand of rightness and justice.

Jeremiah 26:3 -

It may be that they will listen and turn every man from his evil way, that I may relent and reverse My decision concerning the evil which

I purpose to do to them because of their evil doings.

John 8:36 -

So if the Son liberates you [makes you free men], then you are really and unquestionably free.

James 4:8 -

Come close to God and He will come close to you. [Recognize that you are] sinners, get your soiled hands clean; [realize that you have been disloyal] wavering individuals with divided interests, and purify your hearts [of your spiritual adultery].

WHAT IS YOUR PERSONAL RESPONSE?

_____

_____

_____

_____

_____

_____

We are repeatedly told in scripture that if we will turn to God, He will hear us and turn to us.[8] We are reminded that even if we aren't aware of it, He is our God. Not only that, but He says that He will strengthen us, help us, and He will uphold us with the right hand of His righteousness.[9] We are promised that if we will listen to His words, the Bible, and turn from all of our evil ways, He will not give us the judgment and punishment which we've earned and rightly deserve. Jesus promises that if you will come to Him for freedom, your freedom will be true and everlasting freedom from sin and guilt.[10]

In addition, if we seek to draw nearer to God, through Jesus, He will draw nearer to us, purifying our hearts by the regeneration of the Spirit of God, cleansing our hands in the shed blood of the Lamb of God, and giving us minds to serve Him come what may.[11]

In the Old Testament times, they had the Law of Moses to live by. The problem was that no man could ever live it perfectly and, therefore, all were still sinners. God in all His mercy, gave us His only Begotten Son, so that anyone who believes in him would never perish, but have everlasting life![12] The only way to approach God is through His Son. This is good news, since the only requirement is a repentant heart and faith in Him as the Risen Son of God. We have no laws to be stumbling blocks for us.[13]

Anyone who seeks to approach the Father without the Son will find the Son a stumbling block which is impassable.

Luke 20:17 & 18 -

But [Jesus] looked at them and said, "What then is [the meaning of] this that is written: The [very] stone which the builders rejected has become the chief stone of the corner [cornerstone].

Everyone who falls on that stone will be broken [in pieces]; But upon whomever it

*falls, it will crush him [winnow him
and scatter him as dust]*

See also Daniel 2:34-35, Isaiah 8:14-15 and Psalm
118:22-23.

**3. Why am I separated from God without
Jesus?**

John 14:6 -

*Jesus said to him, I am the Way and the
Truth and the Life; no one comes to the Father
except by (through) Me.*

John 6:44 & 45 -

*No one is able to come to Me unless the Father
Who sent Me attracts and draws him and
gives him the desire to come to Me, and [then]
I will raise him up [from the dead] at the last
day. It is written in [the book of] the Prophets,
And they shall all be taught of God [have
Him in person for their Teacher]. Everyone
who has listened to and learned from the
Father comes to Me.*

Luke 19:10 -

*For the Son of Man came to seek and to save
that which was lost.*

John 10:27 & 30 -

*The sheep that are My own hear and are lis-
tening to My voice; and I know them, and they
follow Me. And I give them eternal life, and
they shall never lose it or perish throughout
the ages. [To all eternity they shall never*

by any means be destroyed.] And no one is able to snatch them out of My hand. My Father, Who has given them to Me, is greater and mightier than all [else]; and no one is able to snatch [them] out of the Father's hand. I and the Father are One.

John 6:35 & 37 -

Jesus replied, I am the Bread of Life. He who comes to Me will never be hungry, and he who believes in and cleaves to and trusts in and relies on Me will never thirst any more (at any time).

WHAT IS YOUR PERSONAL RESPONSE?

_____

_____

_____

_____

_____

_____

It seems that this question, "Why am I lost without Jesus Christ?" is one of the most asked when people are confronted with their inadequacy at running their own destiny. The Bible makes the answer very clear as we have just seen. Jesus says that He is the only way to the Father.

• He says that you cannot come to know the Father unless it is through Him.[14]

• He says that all men who learn of the Father come unto Him.[15]

- He says that He (Jesus) came to this world to find
and to save that which is lost (any of us humans who
are sinners).[16]

- Jesus says that if we are His, we know His voice and
we follow Him.[17]

- He offers us eternal life. No man can pluck us out
of His hand.[18]

- He even says that He and the Father (God) are
one.[19]

- What's more, Jesus even tells us that if we come to
Him, we shall never hunger or thirst again.[20]

- In other words, the substance we need to have,
spiritual life (our New Life), is supplied by His word.

Again, Jesus guarantees that if we seek to come to
Him, He will not turn us away no matter what we
have done or where we have been![21] These are
wonderful promises and we can't help but be interested in them, if they are true. The obstacle we face
is inertia; our reluctance to do something new. As
we're about to find out in the next set of scriptures,
this isn't a decision which should be put off.

**4. Why is it so important to respond now;
won't tomorrow do?**

Romans 13:12 & 14 -

*The night is far gone and the day is almost
here. Let us then drop (fling away) the works
and deeds of darkness and put on the [full]
armor of light. Let us live and conduct ourselves honorably and becomingly as in the
[open light of] day, not in reveling (carousing)*

and drunkenness, not in immorality and debauchery (sensuality and licentiousness), not in quarreling and jealousy. But clothe yourself with the Lord Jesus Christ (the Messiah) and make no provision for [indulging] the flesh [put a stop to thinking about the evil cravings of your physical nature] to [gratify its] desires (lusts).

I Thessalonions 5:2 & 3 -

For you yourselves know perfectly well that the day of the [return of the] Lord will come [as unexpectedly and suddenly] as a thief in the night. When people are saying, All is well and secure, and, There is peace and safety then in a moment unforeseen destruction (ruin and death) will come upon them as suddenly as labor pains come upon a woman with child; and they shall by no means escape, for there will be no escape.

II Peter 3:10 -

But the day of the Lord will come like a thief, and then the heavens will vanish (pass away) with a thunderous crash, and the [material] elements [of the universe] will be dissolved with fire, and the earth and the works that are upon it will be burned up.

Revelation 22:7 -

And behold, I am coming speedily. Blessed (happy and to be envied) is he who observes and lays to heart and keeps the truths of the prophecy (the predictions, consolations, and warnings) contained in this little book.

Revelation 22:12 -

Behold, I am coming soon, and I shall bring My wages and rewards with Me, to repay and render to each one just what his own actions and his own work merit.

WHAT IS YOUR PERSONAL RESPONSE?

_____

_____

_____

_____

_____

_____

Can you really afford to gamble with eternity? We have just heard from three different New Testament writers. The message is inescapable, it could be too late at any moment. Paul tells us that we need to discontinue our sinful conduct and to walk in honesty. He tells us that the time for riotous living, drunkenness and other compulsive behavior patterns is running out. We are also warned to put off our tendency towards strife and envy and instead to seek New Life in Christ Jesus. We are to quit attempting to fulfill our lustful natures. We are further warned that the day that the Lord Jesus will return will come unexpectedly. Actually it could be today!

There are no further prophecies to be fulfilled before that day can come, so we should either be looking up in anticipation or looking toward a certain judgment.[22] In the Book of Revelation, Jesus says, *"I come quickly."* He will be bringing everyone what they have coming to them.[23] Those who believe in Him will receive eternal life.[24] Those who deny Him will receive eternal torment in the Lake of Fire.[25] Will you be like the rich man in Luke 12:16-21, or turn in faith now to the only true hope?[26]

It should be noted that the word translated *"believe"* from the original Greek means *"trusts in, clings to, relies on,"* and that when we discuss faith in this book, we will be referring to the original Greek meaning which is used in Galatians 2:20, *"By adherence to and reliance on and complete trust in."*

By now, the need for God in our lives should be apparent. We should have come to believe that we not only need Him, but that He will even help us, unworthy as we are. We have found that without Jesus as our Lord and Savior, we cannot approach God, and we need to respond quickly. If this is where you feel you are, let's proceed to step number three. If you still have doubts or questions, continue to study and pray that Almighty God will open your eyes to the truth of His Living Word.

ADDITIONAL SCRIPTURES

1. Genesis 2:16-17
2. Genesis 3:3
3. Genesis 3:19
4. Isaiah 59:2

5. Romans 6:23 and Proverbs 14:12
6. John 14:6 and Revelation 3:20
7. II Peter 3:9
8. II Chronicles 7:14 and Zechariah 1:3
9. Isaiah 41:10
10. Romans 8:2
11. James 4:8
12. John 3:16
13. Galatians 5:22 & 23
14. John 14:6
15. John 6:45
16. Luke 19:10
17. John 10:27
18. John 10:28
19. John 10:30
20. John 6:35
21. John 6:37
22. Hebrews 10:26-27
23. Revelation 22:12
24. John 3:15
25. Revelation 20:10 & 15 and Revelation 21:8
26. Titus 2:13

STEP THREE

For the better part of my adult life, the idea that I needed to repent seemed ridiculous to me. After all, what did I need to be sorry for and to whom did I owe an apology? Had I done anything that most other people either didn't do or hadn't thought of doing, only lacking the guts to do it? Besides, if I were to go to all the people whom I had wronged or who thought I had wronged them, it would take more than a lifetime to get it done. Not only that, the very people who were the loudest about my need to repent were the ones I thought had the greatest need to repent. How can someone who has no compassion or does nothing to benefit people they can see are hurting, have the gall to tell me I need to repent!

An old rock and roll song kept running through my mind. I think the words were something like this; "He can't even run his own life, I'll be @#!*#@ if he'll run mine!" However, as my life grew progressively more and more unmanageable, I came to realize that since my old ways of thinking and believing didn't seem to work, I was going to have to do something different. Add to that the fear of my quickly approaching death, and I had good motivation for finding something I could believe in. First though, I had to come to grips with this concept of repenting.

Obviously, the concept of a Living God needs to be embraced before it makes any sense to repent. If I were going to repent *(change your mind for the better and heartily amend your ways, with abhorrence of your past sins)*, the admission made in Step Two was necessary. I knew that I needed someone or something more powerful and more capable than I was. Since I had never met anyone who I thought could do a better job of running my life, God was my only hope. Not that I hadn't tried letting others run my life - I had. The problem was that everyone was as bad or worse at knowing what to do than I was. It seemed that others were only capable of doing things for their own good or else they were incapable of understanding my pain.

By this time, I was totally tired of being disappointed by people who were supposedly trying to help, but were in fact, only self-serving. I remember reading something about psychologists and psychiatrists being the most unbalanced group of people and that the profession in general had the highest incidence of alcohol and drug addiction. If I were to go into the details of some of the ideas I received from their counselling this would make a good comedy.

That first morning in church, I had to come to grips with some important questions in a hurry. Praise the Lord, the truth of Scripture which I hadn't even heard before was true (I John 2:26 & 27). Since I was prepared to believe in God as the

Creator of the Universe, obviously I had to approach Him on His own terms. The Bible says that before anything else could or would happen, I had to repent (Luke 13:3).

Okay, I had to accept that, but there were a few questions which I had to work out. First, "Why was I automatically a sinner?" The answer was that Adam sinned and therefore all his descendants were sinners.

That brought up another question, "Why is one man responsible for everyone being a sinner?" Again, the answer was simply that if we turn to one Man (Jesus) for salvation, why should we have such a hard time accepting that one man (Adam) is responsible for sin entering the world?

My next question was, "What if I have committed sins which are unpardonable?" That answer was easy too. Since I still desired forgiveness, I hadn't been guilty of that yet. The Bible says that if we have committed the unpardonable sin, we are given a reprobate mind and no longer desire forgiveness (Romans 1:28-31).

My last question was, "If I will be forgiven for my prior sins, what about any sin that I will commit in the future?" You see, I couldn't conceive not doing anything wrong for the rest of my life. After all, look at the fine mess my life was in now! Again, the answer was easy. The Bible says that in Jesus we have an advocate and intercessor before God, the Father, and He is making intercession for us against the accuser (Satan) (I John 2:1 & 2).

Now that I realized my need for God and my need to repent, I believed that God would not only hear, but would forgive my sins. My next thoughts were to question if there were any special things which I must do first and how I would go about them? Fortunately, I was so desperate that I didn't make the mistake of waiting until I had my life cleaned up before turning to God. What a crock! Some of us have been "getting ourselves ready" for so long that we are stuck in a rut.

There has never before been a time, and there never will be again, that is better than right now, right here, right where you are!

Do we wash up and make sure we are clean before we take a shower or do we make sure that our clothes are clean before we put them in the washing machine? Don't be silly, you say? Don't be fooled by Satan's lies any more, I say! God is waiting for you with open arms, just like the father in the parable of the lost son (Luke 15:11-24); come just as you are, let Him do the cleaning up!

When I took the step of repenting before God, it seemed that a gigantic weight had been taken off my shoulders. The future no longer seemed hopeless or unbearable. This experience cannot be logically explained or proven until you have done it, so I guess that if you are interested in finding out if the relief is real, you'll have to try it for yourself by repenting before God.

The question is, "Has the world kicked you around long enough yet, are you sick and tired of being sick and tired, or do you need to suffer some more before you are willing to admit your need for God and your need to repent? If you are where I was, and know that you need help, all that is stopping you from experiencing true freedom and becoming a member of the family of God, is guts.

Maybe you think that Christians are a bunch of weaklings who need a crutch. You are partially right, we do need a "crutch," His name is Jesus. The part that you apparently haven't understood is that our crutch will not make us sick or kill us. Whatever you have chosen as your crutch will make you sick, it will offer you no hope for a future, either in this life or in the one hereafter! Wise up, look around; do you see the people who are doing what you do with any better reason to live than you have? I didn't think so!

Maybe you feel that I should talk nicer and take it easy, after all, this is a big step. I have a very spiritual reply for you, "Baloney!" I should be coming down harder; your eternity is on the line and the thought of anyone needlessly going to Hell makes me want to vomit! Excuse my language, but I get very adamant about this point. I will not "take it easy;" not only is your eternity on the line, but your future in this life is, too.

Of course, you can put it off for a while longer. The problem is that you have no guarantees that you will have a while longer to think about it. The only guarantee you have is that if you will turn to God in repentance, He will forgive you. Remember, we don't set the date of our own death and when it comes, it is too late to change. You can, of course, be like the dog in Proverbs 26:11 who returns to his own vomit, or like the fool who returns to his own folly!

Do yourself a favor, if you have discovered your need for God, read Psalm 1:1 & 2:

> *Blessed (happy, fortunate, prosperous, and enviable) is the man who walks and lives not in the counsel of the ungodly (following their advice, their plans and purposes), nor stands (submissive and inactive) in the path where sinners walk, nor sits down (to relax and rest) where the scornful (and the mockers) gather. But his delight and desire are in the law of the Lord, and on His law (the precepts, the instructions, the teachings of God) he habitually meditates (ponders and studies) by day and by night.*

What is it going to be? Will you go on with this step and see it through or will you turn tail and run? If you run, you are admitting that after all, you really don't want to change, you are just looking for excuses to justify the miserable condition your choices have caused you to be in.

STEP THREE
REPENT

We repented towards God for our sins and began to trust in His promise that if we repent, we are once for all forgiven.

Today we live in a world of substitutes. Margarine has been substituted for butter, plastic has been substituted for metal, polyester has been substituted for cotton.

We find in "The Open Bible," in the section, "A Guide to Christian Workers," (Thomas Nelson Publishers, 1978, 1979) the following:

Beware, there is no substitute for repentance. *TURNING OVER A NEW LEAF IS NOT REPENTANCE.* Discontinuing a habitual activity by willpower will not bring you any closer to being a son of the Living God. That is like taking aspirin for the headache caused by brain cancer. It might help the symptom, but it does nothing for the cause.

Repentance is always followed by genuine fruit (see Luke 3:8). *PROVING ONE'S MANHOOD IS NOT REPENTANCE.* Men "dead in trespasses and sins" (Ephesians 2:1, NOB) cannot throw back their shoulders and say, "I did it on my own; now I have gained righteousness." Christ's death on the cross for our sins doesn't appeal to our pride, but the fact is that without His atoning death, our repentance would have no effect. Instead of giving us manly pride, the cross exposes man's degradation. The only thing we can offer God (which doesn't stink) is our repentance and faith.

DENYING THE EXISTENCE OF SIN IS NOT REPENTANCE. God, the Creator, doesn't deny sin; the Cross of Calvary is His recognition of sin. One of the first necessary steps towards salvation and the remission of sin is to recognize your need for repentance, not deny it. Satan, one of the chief sources of sin, has done a masterful job in the years since Christ's death at Calvary. One of his best deceptions is to convince us that he doesn't exist. If we don't believe that he exists, then we can be fooled all the more.

Let me offer you a challenge right now; if you don't believe that Satan is real, resist him once, and see what happens. Let me caution you though, if you don't have Jesus living in you and through you, you are likely to get a severe beating. It may not be physical but it will be painful, none-the-less. Keep in mind what the Bible says in John 8:44,

...When he speaketh a lie, he speaketh of his own: for he is a liar, and the father of it (KJV).

Satan is a formidable enemy, but Jesus defeated him openly in Colossians 2:15. When you come to repentance, make sure that you are undertaking to repent for your own sake. Many times we can be tempted to do a thing because it will gain some advantage or because someone we care about wants us to do it. Do this because you have seen the error of your ways and the Spirit of God is convicting you. Paul tells us to work out our own salvation with fear and trembling (Philippians 2:12).

Let's look at what the Bible has to say about some pertinent questions regarding repentance. You are about to embark on a venture that could be the most important step you will ever take. One of my favorite songs says,

The next hand you shake could be
the hand of the Savior,
The next step you take could be
on streets of purest gold,
Your next meal could be
the Marriage supper,
And the next touch you feel He could be
blessing your soul.

Or, would you rather be cast into a lake of fire for all eternity?

1. Why repent before God?

Isaiah 64:6 -

For we have all become like one who is un-clean [ceremonially, like a leper], and all our righteousness (our best deeds of rightness and justice) is like filthy rags or a polluted gar-ment; we all fade like a leaf, and our ini-quities, like the wind, take us away [far from God's favor, hurrying us toward destruction].

Romans 3:20 & 23 -

For no person will be justified (made righteous, acquitted, and judged acceptable) in His sight by observing the works prescribed by the Law. For [the real function of] the Law is to make men recognize and be conscious of sin [not mere perception, but an acquaintance with sin which works toward repentance, faith, and holy character]. Since all have sinned and are falling short of the honor and glory which God bestows and receives.

II Corinthians 5:21 -

For our sake He made Christ [virtually] to be sin Who knew no sin, so that in and through Him we might become [endued with, viewed as being in, and examples of] the righteousness of God [what we ought to be, approved and acceptable and in right relationship with Him, by His goodness].

Revelation 1:17 & 18 -

...I am the First and the Last, And the Everliving One [I Am, living in the eternity of the eternities]. I died, but see, I am alive forevermore; and I possess the keys of death and Hades (the realm of the dead).

WHAT IS YOUR PERSONAL RESPONSE?

_____

_____

_____

_____

_____

We can see that the Bible says that we have no good thing in us and that everything we attempt to do on our own to be righteous, will end in failure. Our attempts at being good are shortlived and poorly conceived at best. The sinful nature which resides in all of us will, in the end, lead us on a path of sure destruction (Proverbs 14:12).

We can't live up to the Law of Moses; no one other than Jesus Christ ever has, so we cannot be considered good enough in God's eyes. The Law of Moses was given to us to point us towards our need for a deliverer (the Greek words used for deliverance and for salvation are often the same).

So, now we know that we fall short of the mark, but what shall we do? We need someone who does qualify in the eyes of God, to be the sacrifice for us.[1]

God, in all His Mercy, sent Jesus to take all of our sins and shortcomings on Himself.[2] Jesus had never sinned and never will, so He is qualified to be that sacrifice. Therefore, we are made positionally righteous in God's eyes. Now, when He looks at those of us who believe in His Son, He sees the righteousness of Jesus instead of our filthy rags. Jesus now is in possession of the keys to Satan's prison houses and snares (Isaiah 42:22), and is standing ready to set free whoever will come into the light.

Remember that God sent Jesus to be born of a virgin woman, to be put to death in shame and rejection on a cross, and to be raised again from the dead so that we may be set free from the bondages of sin.

John 15:13 -

No one has greater love [no one has shown stronger affection] than to lay down (give up) his own life for his friends.[3]

2. How do I know I can trust God?

Psalm 34:8 -

O Taste and see that the Lord [our God] is good! Blessed (happy, fortunate, to be envied) is the man who trusts and takes refuge in Him.

Psalm 103:17-19 -

But the mercy and loving-kindness of the Lord are from everlasting to everlasting upon those who reverently and worshipfully fear Him, and His righteousness is to children's children, To such as keep His covenant [hearing, receiving, loving, and obeying it] and to those who [earnestly] remember His commandments to do them [imprinting them on their hearts]. The Lord has established His throne in the heavens, and His kingdom rules over all.

Matthew 7:7-11 -

Keep on asking and it will be given you, keep on seeking and you will find; keep on knocking [reverently] and [the door] will be opened to you. For everyone who keeps on seeking finds; and to him who keeps on knocking, [the door] will be opened. Or what man is there of you, if his son asks him for a loaf of bread, will hand him a stone? Or if he asks for a fish, will hand him a serpent? If you then, evil as you are, know how to give good and advantageous gifts to your children, how much more will your Father Who is in heaven [perfect as He is] give good and advantageous things to those who keep on asking Him!

John 3:16-17 -

*For God so greatly loved and dearly prized
the world that He [even] gave up His only begotten (unique) Son, so that whoever believes
in (trusts in, clings to, relies on) Him shall not
perish (come to destruction, be lost) but have
eternal (everlasting) life. For God did not
send the Son into the world in order to judge
(to reject, to condemn, to pass sentence on) the
world, but that the world might find salvation and be made safe and sound through
Him.*

WHAT IS YOUR PERSONAL RESPONSE?

_____

_____

_____

_____

_____

_____

As we read earlier, God has never sinned or
tempted anyone to sin. Therefore, His word is the
truth, and we can believe whatever He says. Here
the Bible tells us that the Lord is good. Those of us
who know Him, know that this is the absolute truth.
The only ones who doubt that God is good, are those
who have never become part of His Kingdom. We
also see that "His mercy endureth forever;" this particular statement is repeated forty-one times in the
scriptures. If He repeated it so many times, He must
mean for us to believe it without doubt.

Jesus tells us that:

• anyone who comes to Him, He "will in no wise cast out,"[4]

• that no one can "pluck us from His, or His Father's hand,"[5]

• that if we "seek we will find," if we "knock it will be opened," if we "ask it will be answered,"[6]

• that God is the "giver of all good gifts."[7]

Anything we receive from Him will be perfect for that time and place in our lives. Imagine sending your only son to certain death after a life of suffering and rejection by the very people you sent him to save. Do you love anyone enough to pay that price for them, knowing that they will reject your offer? Could you, after seeing what they did, then offer that same mercy to a group of people who were considered lower than animals? God in His infinite love did exactly that![8]

All we have to do is to turn from ourselves and toward Him in repentance and we, too, can be saved from an eternity of separation from His love in a place of torment that was never designed for men in the first place.[9] Hell was created for Satan and those angels who decided to follow him in rebellion against God.

3. If I repent will God really forgive me?

Proverbs 28:13 -

He who covers his transgressions will not prosper, but whoever confesses and forsakes his sins will obtain mercy.

Psalm 103:12 -

As far as the east is from the west, so far has He removed our transgressions from us.

Acts 3:19 -

So repent (change your mind and purpose); turn around and return [to God], that your sins may be erased (blotted out, wiped clean), that times of refreshing (of recovering from the effects of heat, of reviving with fresh air) may come from the presence of the Lord.

I John 1:9 -

If we [freely] admit that we have sinned and confess our sins, He is faithful and just (true to His own nature and promises) and will forgive our sins [dismiss our lawlessness] and [continuously] cleanse us from all unrighteousness [everything not in conformity to His will in purpose, thought, and action].

WHAT IS YOUR PERSONAL RESPONSE?

_____

_____

_____

_____

_____

_____

Indeed, we can be certain that if we confess our sins, they are forgiven but, conversely, if we don't confess them we can also be certain that they will not be forgiven. We know that the only way to enter into God's Kingdom (Heaven) is to be sinless. Therefore, if we have unconfessed sins.... Get the point?

We are promised that if we do confess, they will be irrevocably removed from God's sight, as far as the east is from the west. We also see that the conversion to become joint heirs with Christ follows confession of our sinful condition. I can think of no greater horror than to stand before the Judgment Seat of the Almighty God only to discover that the repentance we made light of, was actually a very real and necessary part of salvation.

We just saw the time of His second coming referred to as a time of refreshment. Praise God, who would be foolish enough to want torment as opposed to refreshment? God is truly faithful, even when we are not. God is omnipotent, omniscient, and omnipresent.

• He is all powerful (nothing is impossible for Him)[10]

• He knows all things (He knew the end before the beginning)[11]

• He is everywhere at once and sees everything, both hidden and open.[12]

> *Thus saith the Lord God: I have no pleasure in the death of the wicked. But that the wicked turn from his way and live: Turn you, turn you, from your evil ways; for why will you die? (Ezekiel 33:11).*

4. How do I repent?

II Chronicles 7:14 -

If My people, who are called by My name, shall humble themselves, pray, seek, crave, and require of necessity My face and turn from their wicked ways, then will I hear from heaven, forgive their sin, and heal their land.

Psalm 51:15-17 -

O Lord, open my lips, and my mouth shall show forth Your praise. For You delight not in sacrifice, or else would I give it; You find no pleasure in burnt offering. My sacrifice [the sacrifice acceptable] to God is a broken spirit; a broken and a contrite heart [broken down with sorrow for sin and humbly and thoroughly penitent], such, O God, You will not despise.

Psalm 34:18 -

The Lord is close to those who are of a broken heart and saves such as are crushed with sorrow for sin and are humbly and thoroughly penitent.

II Corinthians 7:10 -

For godly grief and the pain God is permitted to direct, produce a repentance that leads and contributes to salvation and deliverance from evil, and it never brings regret; but worldly grief (the hopeless sorrow that is characteristic of the pagan world) is deadly [breeding and ending in death].

WHAT IS YOUR PERSONAL RESPONSE?

_____

_____

_____

_____

_____

   The HOW of repentance is actually very simple,
just as the entire gospel of salvation is simple. We,
that is mankind in general, like to make everything
complex and difficult. More than likely this is because we feel somehow more intelligent or like someone more important if we appear to have done
something that is hard to figure out or hard to do.

   That couldn't be farther from the truth; Jesus, by
His vicarious, atoning death on the cross has already
proven that each of us is absolutely special and important, by that act of love. All we need to do is confess our sins and our sinful nature. The condition of
this confession will necessarily be a broken or "contrite" heart.[13] The reason for this, is that in order
for man to admit his abominable condition he must
be literally broken.[14] Until that point is reached, we
are too proud and full of ourselves. In both Old and
New Testaments, we are continually told that if
God's people will repent, He will hear, forgive, heal,
restore, deliver, and more![16]

   God isn't interested in our vain attempts at good
works, in our efforts to be good enough, in our ability
to always point a finger at someone else who either

is to blame or is worse than we are. He is interested
in our turning to Him. It matters not where you are
physically when you repent. You could be walking,
sitting, riding in a car or bus, laying down, or even
kneeling down at an altar in a church. If the Spirit
of God is convicting you of your need for repentance
and salvation, won't you turn now to the Almighty
God? He is waiting for you and has nothing but His
unending love waiting, if you will just turn to Him.
As the last scripture we just quoted says, we have a
choice of sorrows. Will you choose Godly sorrow or
worldly sorrow? You already know how much good
worldly sorrow does, why not try Godly sorrow and
you, too, can "taste and see that the Lord is good"
(Psalm 34:8a). Will you trust Him, and be blessed
with His righteous forgiveness, or will you continue
to deny Him and be cursed with his righteous judgment?

ADDITIONAL SCRIPTURES

1. Ephesians 5:2
2. John 3:16-17
3. John 15:13
4. John 6:37
5. John 10:28-29
6. Luke 11:9
7. James 1:17
8. Matthew 15:22-28

9. Matthew 25:41
10. Luke 1:37
11. Isaiah 46:10
12. Jeremiah 23:24
13. Psalm 34:18
14. Psalm 51
15. Hosea 6:1b

STEP FOUR

Many times during the decline and fall of my life, people told me, "If you would be born again, you would find a whole new life." If I had ever read the Bible, I would have repeated the question in John 3:1-12.

I hadn't though, so my answer was not exactly as nicely worded as the one Nicodemus gave. When people would tell me I needed to be born again, I usually replied, "Don't be stupid; what am I supposed to do, crawl back inside my mother?" (expletives deleted). In fact, my resistance to the Gospel was such that when people witnessed to me there was always a loud argument and, at times, a one-sided fist fight, if they didn't shut up and go away.

Remember when the "Jesus Freaks" were on every street corner asking people if they had talked to the Lord? Keep in mind that "bikers" didn't have any fondness for "hippies," so can you imagine how I would react to some spaced-out hippie with green teeth and stringy hair, telling me that he had the answer to my problems. Why would someone who was as intelligent and capable (right, a strung-out loser) as I was, want something that was for weak creeps who couldn't handle being responsible for their own lives?

"Born again," who could know what that meant? There were other times, when people tried to tell me of the wonder-working power of the Lord, that I personally tried to destroy their faith. I remember a time when I was in a group therapy program (psychiatric) in which one of the members was a brand new Christian. He would try to tell us that he had found real help and freedom, and I would spend hours telling him what a fool he was! Like I always said, I was a prime candidate for God's love.

There are many examples of those kinds of behavior towards others who were trying to tell me of a truth which I was afraid to hear. Many of us try to put on a front of self-sufficiency and strength, when the real truth is that we are afraid to:

a) Admit our fear of relinquishing control of our lives to something we cannot understand, and

b) Admit our total fear of doing something out of the ordinary and being mocked or scorned by our "friends."

Many times the decision is made not to turn to God because a person cannot stand the thought of being different from the herd. The people we call friends are actually just acquaintances who will be there as long as we can benefit them. What we don't realize is that Jesus is a friend who is always there, even in our darkest hour when the real truth of our lives is revealed.

After quite a few years of people trying to get me to listen, I began to wonder if maybe there was something to this that I didn't understand. Until I had listened to the Gospel of Jesus Christ, and accepted it as the truth, I couldn't understand what the Bible said. Like Jesus said in John 3:5 & 6:

...I assure you, most solemnly I tell you, unless a man is born of water and [even] the Spirit, he cannot [ever] enter the kingdom of God. What is born of [from] the flesh is flesh [of the physical is physical]; and what is born of the spirit is spirit.

He was speaking a "mystery." The "mystery" is not fathomable in the natural realm in which we live. The only way to understand it is to be a part of it. Imagine yourself sitting facing a window with a beautiful sunset showing through it. Now imagine that there is someone who has never seen a sunset or the colors in one, sitting facing you, with his back to the window. Is there any way to explain to this person what you are seeing? No, the only way that person can understand the beautiful scene you see, is if he will turn and look at it for himself!

This is the "mystery of the Gospel." We have had a veil placed over our vision which prevents us from seeing the truth of the Gospel of Christ. It cannot be adequately described or understood until we turn in faith towards God, to look at the beauty of the Kingdom of God with our own regenerated spiritual eyes (please read II Corinthians 3:14-16).

No doubt many who read this will scoff and say, "How dumb do you think I am? Why should I believe something that I cannot see or understand?" I can only say, "How will you know if I am telling you a truth that you can't comprehend, if you don't try it for yourself?"

Up to the very moment that I met the Living Lord, I was full of doubt and questions. I remember thinking on my way to the altar, "This cannot work; there is no way that I'll ever be well physically or emotionally. How could God accept someone as full of sin as I am; someone whom I hate above all others?" My mind was still full of cursing; hatred still reigned supreme; I needed to get high so I could quit hurting. I was sure that this, too, would turn out to be an exercise in futility. There had been so many false starts and false hopes, I had no faith to believe that anything could ever change me for good.

Fortunately, being "born again" doesn't depend on our own faith to make it happen. If the Spirit of God is drawing us, we will be born again. If we had to have faith that it was real before we could be born again, we wouldn't need to be born again. I would like to take a few moments to relate the experience I had the first time I heard and responded to the Gospel.

We had gone to the First Assembly of God Church in Cerritos, California, at the urging of the new friends I spoke of in an earlier chapter. There were about three or four hundred people there and Linda and I didn't know what to expect. I remember when someone spoke in an unknown tongue and someone else translated it, I turned to Linda and said, "Do they rehearse that?" Many things that I didn't understand were happening, the most exciting of them on the inside of me! The only things that I knew for sure that morning were that I was desperate (remember the requirement for repentance, being broken?), and that the man who was the preacher (Pastor Ed Rutherford) believed what he was saying.

The service evidently wasn't going as they normally do, as I learned later. After about an hour of singing, the Pastor got up in front and said that he had a beautiful sermon ready, but he believed that the Spirit of God wanted everyone just to worship that day. After about another hour, the Pastor got up again and said that the Lord had just spoken to him and that there was someone there that day who had no hope and was sick to death. Then he said that if that person would come forward for prayer, right that moment, that the Lord would move in a great and mighty way.

I don't know if there was anyone else there who was in that condition, but I knew he was talking to me. I may have been sick and hopeless, but even in my sickness I could tell when someone was telling the truth as they perceive it. In any case, I grabbed Linda's hand and said, "I don't know if you agree, but you are coming with me." As we started down that aisle, things began to happen! Before we got to the front, I was no longer aware that I was in a building or that there were any other people there. I don't know where I was, but it was spectacular!

The next thing I remember was that the hatred and pain I had always known was gone and I seemed to be about to explode with excitement. Instead of being scared by all this, it somehow seemed a comfort; there was a growing peace which I had never known before. I know that the Pastor prayed with me, but I have no idea what we prayed, or what he said; the experiences that were going through my entire being had my complete attention.

After some time had passed, I noticed that the service was apparently over. As I stood there, I began to marvel that the cursing in my mind was gone and my whole thought process had changed. After years of only thinking of myself, I was thinking of what I could do to show the Lord my gratitude for the wonderful work He had begun that morning. Most of what went on that morning is beyond my ability to express with words, but I know that Jesus will be just as real to anyone who sincerely desires to be born again, and is being drawn by the Spirit of God as He was to me.

Unfortunately, not everyone who is born again is going to go through such a dramatic first-time experience, but everyone who is born again comes to know the glory of the Lord's love in an intimate way. Is this for you? Is the Spirit of God drawing you right now? Only you know, but if He is, go for it! You will never find anything as powerful and life-changing as the Living Lord.

Will you ask Jesus to come into your heart and life today, or will you continue to search for things to fill the emptiness you are experiencing in places that

will only cause you more pain and grief? Only you
can make that decision!

STEP FOUR

BE BORN AGAIN

**We requested that Jesus come into our
hearts and lives that we may be born again
as He said we would be.**

*Therefore if any man be in Christ, he is a new
creature: Old things are passed away; behold, all things are become new. (KJV)*

Being born again, carries with it life-changing
and far-reaching implications. It signifies a new
beginning. Think of it, a chance to start over. Many
of us have attempted to start over. We moved to new
towns, we got new friends, we have even left one
mate and found another hoping to find the right
combination. The problem is that wherever we went,
the same people were there. They may have had different faces and different names, but they were the
same people, weren't they?

In the new towns we tried, we found the
same hangouts and the same places we thought we
had left. Our new mates proved to be only a different type of problem, but still a problem. The issue
we can't sidestep, no matter how hard we try or
where we go is that, wherever we go, we always
find ourselves there.

It isn't the people around us, the places we live, the circumstances we are in, our mothers or fathers, our wives or husbands, our children or even our past that is our worst enemy. It is us! To quote a line from a cartoon, "We have met the enemy, and 'they is us.'" Someone once told me that if I ever found the perfect place to live, I'd ruin it. That was a little hard to understand until I took a "no excuses" look at myself. We do indeed need a "new life" but we will not find it in the natural realm which we can see. Our only hope is to find peace with God. People often have told me that they can find their own peace, without God, on their own terms. If that deception were true, there wouldn't be so many of us running around who can't even find our back pockets with both hands.

The answer is so simple and easy to find that we will try almost everything else first. We ask, "How can something I can't see, hear, feel, or even know for sure exists, help me? There must be something that I have to do first." Actually there is. We discussed it in the last step. We have to repent [change your mind for the better, heartily amend your ways, with abhorrance of your past sins] of our sins and ask God to give us His new birth. Do you find that a little hard to swallow? After all, nothing else has ever caused us to change. To those of us who have taken that step, the thing that is hardest to understand is why anyone would ever refuse to try it!

Another excuse we often hear is that it would mean giving up too much. I will use my theological word again for that, "Baloney!" In truth, there are things which will have to be given up, the following is a partial list:

- Being sick of life and sick of yourself, as well as sick physically.
- Waking up wondering where you are and how you got there.
- Waiting for someone to pay your bail.
- Having only friends who use you and can't be trusted.
- Degradation and shame at the way you live.
- Failing at everything you try and ruining everything you touch.
- Getting beat up or beating someone else up for no reason.
- Being alone, even in a crowded bar.
- Not even knowing what the truth is, you've lied so much.
- Being turned away by people who once loved you.
- Knowing that tomorrow will only be worse than today.
- Knowing that dreams are for fools, they never come true.

Do any of those fit you? If they do, I have a friend that will help you change all of them. His name is Jesus, He is waiting at the door of your heart.

Cast your burden on the Lord [releasing the weight of it] and He will sustain you; He will never allow the [consistently] righteous to be

moved (made to slip, fall, or fail) (Psalm
55:22).

"Can this really be true?" you say; "Why don't you
find out for yourself," I say! That is the only way you
will ever know for sure. We can speculate and
philosophize forever and never know for sure. Go on
with this step if we have said something which
makes you want to know more. You never know,
your entire future may be on the line!

**1. If I ask Him, will Jesus come into my
heart?**

John 3:17 -

*For God did not send the Son into the world
in order to judge (to reject, to condemn, to
pass sentence on) the world, but that the
world might find salvation and be made safe
and sound through Him.*

Revelation 3:20 -

*Behold, I stand at the door and knock: if
anyone hears and listens to and heeds My
voice and opens the door, I will come in to him
and will eat with him, and he [will eat] with
Me.*

Revelation 22:17 -

*The [Holy] Spirit and the bride (the church,
the true Christians) say, Come! And let him
who is listening say Come! And let
everyone come who is thirsty [who is
painfully conscious of his need of those things
by which the soul is refreshed, supported, and*

*stengthened]; and whoever [earnestly] desires
to do it, let him come, take, appropriate, and
drink the water of Life without cost.*

John 6:35 & 37 -

*Jesus replied, I am the Bread of Life. He who
comes to Me will never be hungry, and he who
believes in and cleaves to and trusts in and
relies on Me will never thirst any more (at any
time). All whom My Father gives (entrusts) to
Me will come to Me; and the one who comes to
Me I will most certainly not cast out [I will
never, no never, reject one of them who comes
to Me].*

WHAT IS YOUR PERSONAL RESPONSE?

_____
_____
_____
_____
_____
_____

Obviously, we need to know that if we ask Jesus
to enter and take over our lives, He will do it.[1] His
unfailing love for us in our fallen state must be assured. Spiritually, we are born again when we drink
the water of life. We have here not only the promise
that He will come in, but that he will sit down and
eat with us.[2] This is important in the context of the
time it was written.

In Hebrew society, if you entered a person's house
it was one thing, but to eat with them was yet

another. It signified your acceptance of the person as one worthy of fellowship. The most exciting news is that no matter who we are, where we've been, what we've done or said, if the Spirit of God is drawing us to confess[3] and we ask Jesus to be our Savior, He (Jesus) will not cast us out or exclude us from His fellowship.[4]

Once we have been "born again", and have been sealed by the Spirit of God,[5] our "New Life" can begin. The changes can be staggering as well as exciting. Right now, you should be wondering what "born again" means. You might also have some fears that you will be required to do something outlandish. Don't worry, the dramatic and life-changing things which are in store for you will begin on the inside and will require that you do nothing that the Spirit of God doesn't lead you to do.[6]

2. What does born again mean?

Ezekiel 36:26 -

A new heart will I give you and a new spirit will I put within you, and I will take away the stony heart out of your flesh and give you a heart of flesh.

I Peter 1:23 -

You have been regenerated (born again), not from a mortal origin (seed, sperm), but from one that is immortal by the ever living and lasting Word of God.

Titus 3:5 -

He saved us, not because of any works of righteousness that we had done, but because of His own pity and mercy, by [the] cleansing [bath] of the new birth (regeneration) and renewing of the Holy Spirit.

John 1:12 & 13 -

But to as many as did receive and welcome Him, He gave the authority (power, privilege, right) to become the children of God, that is, to those who believe in (adhere to, trust in and rely on) His name - Who owe their birth neither to bloods nor to the will of the flesh [that of physical impulse] nor to the will of man [that of a natural father], but to God. [They are born of God!].

I John 5:1 -

Everyone who believes (adheres to, trusts, and relies on the fact) that Jesus is the Christ (the Messiah) is a born-again child of God; and everyone who loves the Father also loves the one born of Him (His offspring).

WHAT IS YOUR PERSONAL RESPONSE?

_____
_____
_____
_____
_____
_____

When we speak of our heart, we are not speaking about the muscle in our chests which pumps blood. We are talking about the essence which is you. When the Word of God says that we will receive a new heart, it is not saying that we will receive a new muscle to pump blood. What is meant is that we will receive a washing and regeneration, accompanied by a renewing of our spirit.[7] Without this process there still would be no room for any hope or for the truth in our lives. In other words, we need to be made clean so that we can be infused with the truth of the Gospel of Jesus Christ.

Being "born again" is the process by which we are given the spiritual life which was forfeited by Adam in the Garden. This time, we are not conceived in sin and born in sin (Psalms 51:5), but we are born of the Word of God.[8] This life is everlasting and as such, will not be characterized like the Bob Dylan song which says, "Everyone who is not busy being born is busy dying." This life is in and through Jesus.

Now we are truly joint heirs, not born by some random sexual act or even by the desire of a couple who wanted children. There won't necessarily be any physical changes or any outward evidence, this birth is by the *agape* love of God (see II Peter 3:9). Remember, our filthy rags cannot save us, only the infinite mercy of a loving God who sent His Son to die for a world of lost sinners. What will you choose - the love of His Son, or the hatred of Satan?

3. What are the results when I am born again?

II Corinthians 5:17 -

Therefore if any person is [ingrafted] in Christ (the Messiah) he is a new creation (a new creature altogether); the old [previous moral and spiritual condition] has passed away. Behold, the fresh and new has come!

Galatians 5:22-25 -

But the fruit of the [Holy] Spirit [the work which His presence within accomplishes] is love, joy (gladness), peace, patience (an even temper, forbearance), kindness, goodness (benevolence), faithfulness, gentleness (meekness, humility), self-control (self-restraint, continence). Against such things there is no law [that can bring a charge]. And those who belong to Christ Jesus (the Messiah) have crucified the flesh (the godless human nature) with its passions and appetites and desires. If we live by the [Holy] Spirit, let us also walk by the Spirit. [If by the Holy Spirit we have our life in God, let us go forward walking in line, our conduct controlled by the Spirit.]

John 11:25 & 26 -

Jesus said to her, I am [Myself] the Resurrection and the Life. Whoever believes in (adheres to, trusts in, and relies on) Me, although he may die, yet he shall live; And whoever continues to live and believes in (has faith in, cleaves to, and relies on)

Me shall never [actually] die at all. Do you believe this?

John 10:10 -

The thief comes only in order to steal and kill and destroy. I came that they may have and enjoy life, and have it in abundance (to the full, till it overflows).

WHAT IS YOUR PERSONAL RESPONSE?

_____
_____
_____
_____
_____
_____

Is there anyone who wouldn't willingly rid himself of the character flaws that we all have? Yet when Jesus made that very offer, we (that is the human race) said, "No!" The Bible says that *"old things are passed away and all things are made new."*[9] Perhaps part of the problem is that some of those who claim to be Christians have held on to major portions of their lives.

For some reason many people try to make a deal with the Lord. The problem is that He doesn't make deals. We can't say to the Lord, "OK Lord, You take care of all the big things and I'll take care of the little ones." If we do that, pretty soon everything is a "little one" and there is no room for the Lord in our lives. We pray for the Lord to help us or to deliver us and yet we refuse to get out of the way. I once heard a man who was having some major problems in his life say, "Listen here young man, I've been in The Way for forty years." His pastor calmly replied, "That is probably a large portion of the problem."

We must never forget who our enemy is; Satan is described vividly in John 10:10; the Bible also says that he goes about like a roaring lion seeking whom he may devour (I Peter 5:8).

4. How can I know that I am really born again?

Titus 1:2 -

[Resting] in the hope of eternal life, [life] which the ever truthful God who cannot deceive promised before the world or the ages of time began.

I John 3:24 -

All who keep His commandments [who obey His orders and follow His plan, live and continue to live, to stay and] abide in Him, and He in them. [They let Christ be a home to them and they are the home of Christ.] And by this we know and understand and have the proof that He [really] lives and makes His home in us: by the [Holy] Spirit Whom He has given us.

John 13:35 -

By this shall all [men] know that you are My disciples, if you love one another [if you keep on showing love among yourselves].

I Corinthians 6:11 -

And such some of you were [once]. But you were washed clean (purified by a complete atonement for sin and made free from the guilt of sin), and you were consecrated (set apart, hallowed), and you were justified [pronounced righteous, by trusting] in the name of the Lord Jesus Christ and in the [Holy] Spirit of our God.

WHAT IS YOUR PERSONAL RESPONSE?

_____
_____
_____
_____
_____
_____

When we want to find out if we really were "born again," there are some fairly clearcut questions which we can ask of ourselves. The character of a changed life will be different than the character which our old lives presented. When you are taking inventory of your own life, don't be disappointed if you don't meet all of these statements as well as you expect you should. Remember that Christian growth is an ongoing process, not a one-time event. Some things may take awhile to filter out from your inner depths. The work of the Spirit of God is done on the inside and doesn't always show immediately in all of its aspects. The following are some of the ways this changed life will show up:

- **We love Christ Jesus.** Before conversion we might have held Christ in high regard, but after conversion, we will love Him as our Lord and Savior (I John 5:1 & 2).
- **We love to talk to God.** Prayer addressed to our Father is a facet of our lives that we miss if we neglect it (Ephesians 5:19, Romans 8:26).
- **We love to read the Bible.** We should feed our souls daily on the Living Word of God, and love the Word as the Psalmist did (Psalm 119:24, 40, 47, 38, 72, 97, 103, 111, 113, 127, 129, 140, 143, 159, 162, 165, 168).
- **We love other Christians.** *"We know that we have passed from death into life, because we love the brethren"* (I John 3:14).
- **We love the pure life.** We have discovered that the freedom offered by Jesus isn't the freedom to do what we want, but the freedom not to do the things that we don't want (I John 5:4 & I John 2:15-17).
- **We love the souls of all people.** Like Paul, we too can cry out for the conversion of our loved ones (Romans 10:1 & II Corinthians 5:14)
- **We love our enemies.** We must follow Matthew 5:43-45.

The above list is not complete but will serve as a helpful checklist for your continuing growth in the Lord Jesus. Remember however, what Paul said in II Corinthians 8:12, in our service to the Lord, as in our giving, a willing heart is as important as our performance. See also Matthew 25:23 & Luke 17:10.

When you've given your best for the Master,
the best your life can afford,
He will say, "well done," to His servant;
"now enter the Joy of the Lord."
- Unknown

IN GOD'S SERVICE, OUR GREATEST ABILITY IS OUR AVAILABILITY!

The following is a description of what we can expect to happen when we are "born again" and pray a sinner's prayer for salvation. If you have never really accepted Jesus as your Savior, do it now!

• We are born again spiritually by the Holy Spirit of God (John 3:3-6).

• We agree with God that we are sinners (Romans 3:23).

• All our sins are forgiven (I John 1:9).

• Jesus comes into our hearts (Revelation 3:20).

• We pass out of death into life (John 5:24).

• We become children of God (John 1:12).

• God puts the Spirit of Jesus in our hearts (Galatians 4:6).

• We know without a doubt we are God's children (Romans 8:16).

• We know we have eternal life (I John 5:11-13).

• Jesus will never leave us nor forsake us (Hebrews 13:5).

- No one can take us out of Jesus' hand (John 10:27, 28)
- The Holy Spirit will be with us forever (John 14:16).
- We have been sealed by the Holy Spirit (Ephesians 1:13 & 4:30).
- We will not be judged (John 3:18, 5:24 & Romans 8:1, 2).
- We have the power of the Holy Spirit to love and have a sound mind (II Timothy 1:7).
- We have the power to win souls for the Lord (Romans 1:16, Acts1:8).

GOD IS GLORIFIED WHEN:

- A Christian bears much fruit (wins people for Jesus) (John 15:8).
- The fruit of the Christian is a tree of life and he who wins souls is wise (Proverbs 11:30).
- God has prepared their hearts, all we have to do is pray with them (John 6:44).

Are you ready right now to pray with me?

Dear God, I am a sinner (Romans 3:23 & Psalm 51:5).
Forgive me of my sins (I John 1:9).
Lord Jesus, come into my heart (Revelation 3:20).
Give me new life (John 6:63 & II Corinthians 3:6).
Thank you, Jesus, for dying on the cross for my sins (I Corinthians 15:3,4).
In Jesus' name, Amen! (John 16:24).

As you can see, we were praying the Word of God and agreeing together in it, and *"When two agree, they can walk together"* (Amos 3:3 & Romans 10:17).

WELCOME TO YOUR NEW FAMILY, GOD BLESS YOU!!

WATER BAPTISM

Now that you have accepted Jesus Christ as your personal Savior, you will have a desire to tell the world about The Lord. One of the ways that you can do this is presented in the Word of God as water baptism. In Mark 16:16, it says this, *"He that believeth and is baptized shall be saved."* This scripture also continues with this statement, *"But he that believeth not shall be damned."*

Baptism is an ordinance of the New Testament Church. It is our memorial testifying to the fact of Christ's crucifixion and resurrection from the dead. Many have asked, "What does baptism mean (or symbolize)?" We will find the answer in the following scriptures:

Romans 6:3-8 -

Are you ignorant of the fact that all of us who have been baptized into Christ Jesus were baptized into His death? We were buried therefore with Him by baptism into death, so that just as Christ was raised from the dead by the glorious [power] of the Father, so we too might [habitually] live and behave in newness of life. For if we have become one with Him by sharing a death like His, we shall also be [one with Him in sharing] His resurrection [by a new life lived for God]. We know that our old (unrenewed) self was nailed to the cross with Him in order that [our] body [which is the instrument] of sin might be made ineffective and inactive for evil, that we might no longer be the slaves of sin. For when a man dies, he is freed (loosed, delivered) from [the power of] sin [among men]. Now if we have died with Christ, we believe that we shall also live with Him.

Water baptism also represents three outstanding events:

First - The death, burial and resurrection of Christ.

Second - A death to sin and a burial of the old nature.

Third - A spiritual resurrection on the part of those accepting Christ.

In II Corinthians 5:17, which you will find used more than once in this book, the Word of God confirms this principle:

Therefore if any person is [ingrafted] in Christ (the Messiah) he is a new creation (a new creature altogether): The old [previous moral and spiritual condition] has passed away. Behold, the fresh and new has come!

From the time we accept Christ, we begin to live a changed life. The things we once thought that we loved and cherished are now unimportant and forgotten. The Christian will no longer love sin or sinful ways. All of his affections are turned toward God and His Kingdom. Paul shares this same message in Galatians 5:24-25,

> And those who belong to Christ Jesus (the Messiah) have crucified the flesh (the godless human nature) with its passions and appetites and desires. If we live by the [Holy] Spirit, let us also walk by the Spirit. [If by the Holy Spirit we have our life in God, let us go forward walking in line, our conduct [controlled by the Spirit].

For the "born again" person, water baptism has a double meaning. It not only becomes a means by which we may make a public expression of our acceptance of Christ as our personal Savior. It also symbolizes the forgiveness of sin through our faith in the sacrificial death of Christ at Calvary.

Jesus died for the sins of men, was buried, and three days later was resurrected. The converted sinner dies a spiritual death to his sin nature, through repentance, buries the old life in the water of baptism, and rises in the likeness of His (Jesus Christ's) resurrection.

Another question commonly asked is, "Why is water baptism required for a born again Christian?" Again, the answers wait for us in the scriptures of the Holy Bible. The Word of God has many examples of conversions and baptisms. With the conversion, that person's baptism is also recorded. Jesus thought it so necessary to be baptized in water that He walked approximately sixty miles to be baptized by John the Baptist.

It says, in Matthew 3:13,

> *Then Jesus came from Galilee to the Jordan to John to be baptized by him.*

That journey would have been about sixty miles, either on foot or by camel or donkey. Is baptism important? Jesus thought so! Acts 2:38 says,

> *And Peter answered them, Repent (change your views and purpose to accept the will of God in your inner selves instead of rejecting it) and be baptized, every one of you, in the name of Jesus Christ for the forgiveness of and release from your sins; and you shall receive the gift of the Holy Spirit,*

We find a similar command in Matthew 28:19-20, this time stated by our Lord, Christ Jesus,

> *Go then and make disciples of all the nations, baptizing them into the name of the Father and of the Son and of the Holy Spirit.*

The Lord is challenging us to win the lost to Him, baptizing them in water, in the name of the Father, Son and Holy Spirit. In the next verse, Jesus promises us that we will have Him to draw strength and wisdom from, no matter where He leads us,

...I am with you all the days (perpetually, uniformly, and on every occasion), to the [very] close and consummation of the age...

In a marriage ceremony, we have a man and a woman who love each other and have chosen to forsake all others, joining themselves together. They have decided to have each other as lifelong companions, until death parts them. At least, that is the way God ordained it. We, today, seem to take the marriage vows somewhat less seriously than the Lord does! This marriage ceremony is a public confession of their love for each other and of their decision to live together for the rest of their lives. They already knew that they loved each other, and wanted to be together, but the ceremony is for the benefit of everyone else. The ceremony is a public announcement of their intention to make the union of their lives according to godly conditions and the laws of the land. Therefore, the ceremony is a witness to the world of their love and devotion.

So it is with water baptism; a sinner hears the voice of Jesus calling, "Give me your heart and life," and he soon finds himself being drawn to Christ by the cords of love. He learns to love Jesus because Jesus first loved him, and gave His life as a ransom for him. Since Christ has already expressed His love *("No one has greater love [no one has shown stronger affection] than to lay down (give up) his own life for his friends")* for sinners, they may now, in return, accept Him as their Savior. Therefore, water baptism is the public ceremony of the union between Jesus Christ and you!

If you need more proof of the need for water baptism, pray to the Father that he may give you wisdom (James 1:5). If that still isn't enough, go back to your initial moment of salvation and check it for validity!

ADDITIONAL SCRIPTURES

1. John 3:16 and I John 2:27
2. Revelation 3:20
3. John 6:44
4. John 6:37
5. Ephesians 1:13
6. Ezekiel 36:27
7. Titus 3:5
8. I Peter 1:23
9. II Corinthians 5:17

STEP FIVE

Imagine if you will, having an acquaintance with whom you have partied, chased women, committed crimes, done drugs and everything else imaginable, and the next time you see him, he is rejoicing about having a personal Savior. That is exactly what the people who knew me experienced beginning the day Linda and I were saved. No doubt, most thought that we had gone off the deep end. That day after we left the church where we were saved, we started calling everyone we knew. Some were glad to hear it, and even though they were rather skeptical about me, they were able to believe that Linda could change.

One old friend told us some time later that she had been asking her church to pray for Linda for years and when they would ask if Linda was married she would say, "Yes, but her husband is so bad that there isn't really much hope for him." Praise God, "His Mercy endureth forever;" the Lord didn't believe that I was beyond help. Some of our friends (those who weren't born again) were quick either to laugh it off or to ridicule us. Some seemed not to be able to get away from us quickly enough, like we had some disease that they could catch.

In any case, we were not to be discouraged. We
kept on calling, kept on telling everyone who would
listen, of the wonder-working power of God. Right
after church, we went to a friend's house to a Super
Bowl party. Looking back, it seems a little comical to
remember myself at a party with a bunch of people
who were drinking and doing cocaine while I was
telling them about Jesus. Obviously, most didn't
want to hear but some did, and some are saved
today.

Most of them spent time trying to get me to have
a drink or do a little coke. I was absolutely shocked
to realize that I had no desire for any of it. There was
no battle and the temptation was not nearly strong
enough to get me to do any of it. In the past, all it
would take was for somebody to offer me any of it
and I would be off and running.

After the party, we began calling again and going
to visit our friends. The strangest part was that the
ones who had been the most adamant about the fact
that I was a mess, were the last to want to hear of
our new lives. We received comments like, "Oh no,
you're not one of those Holy Rollers now are you?"
Or, "We knew you needed help, but now you've gone
totally off the track." Then there was, "What do you
need that junk for?" My favorite was, "Check back
with me in six months when this is all over and you
want to party again." That one was my favorite as
it serves as a constant reminder of my decision to follow Christ.

We were excited because we had seen the truth
and the truth had set us free (John 8:32). We were

free from all of the bondages which held us trapped for so many years. Our new found freedom was, in truth, the freedom to not do the things which we did not want to do, but were powerless otherwise to stop.

When I went to work the next day, I was still rejoicing about the miracle I had experienced. Naturally, some of the people I worked with were more than skeptical. After all, we had partied together every day prior to this and they continued, for quite a while, to ask me to join them after work to get high. Finally, they gave up trying to get me to join them and mostly just tried to embarrass me with statements like, "Look out, here comes the preacher, watch what you say, he may want to pray for you!"

Even though they saw the change in me, most of them weren't in the least bit interested in what the Lord had to offer. Finally, a few weeks later the Sales Manager called me in to tell me that if I wouldn't shut up about Jesus while I was at work, they would have to let me go. That really shocked me as I had been the Salesman of the Month for the previous three months and the man talking to me claimed to be a Christian!

Even that turned out to be a blessing as it gave me the opportunity to spend some time in intensive study of God's word. In case you missed it, I didn't shut up about Jesus, and I never will. If we have been saved from certain and eternal death, from a lifetime of misery now and for an eternity, shouldn't

we want to shout it from the roof tops? I
couldn't understand how these people could help
but be convinced. I am glad though, that I
didn't fall into the trap of going along with them
while they were partying to "convert" them
(Proverbs 13:20).

Don't let Satan fool you into thinking that you can
"handle it now" (whatever you have had problems
handling), because you have the Lord. While your
deliverance is still brand new you should guard it as
though your very life depended on it; it actually may!
Even though our rejoicing didn't have an immediate,
noticeable effect on those around us, we didn't stop.

First of all, some of those we thought weren't listening have since come to know the Lord. What if
we had kept our testimony to ourselves (see Ezekiel
33:2-6). Second, and just as important, by continuing
in praise and rejoicing, we were keeping the joy of
our salvation fresh in our hearts and minds during a
critical time in our walk with the Lord. We didn't
want to be like the seed which was thrown on the
road, among the rocks, or among the thorns (Luke
8:5-7).

When we become Christians, Satan attempts to
use every weapon in his arsenal to trip us up or
destroy our testimony so that we will think we are
useless to the Lord. Sometimes it seemed to Linda
and me that rejoicing was nearly impossible as our
circumstances were apparently not anything to
rejoice about. However, Paul said, "Rejoice ever-
more" and, "Rejoice in the Lord always, and again I
say rejoice." We discovered that one of the best ways

to get through what looks like hard times is to rejoice about our Lord. Not only does the severity of our circumstances begin to look less terrible, but the time until the circumstances change doesn't seem to drag as much.

When we are looking for something to hold onto in a crisis, we are more likely to listen to someone who is excited and happy than to someone who is all down in the mouth and as miserable as we are. You guessed it, we need to be showing our conversion with our life as well as with our mouth. I have found over and over again, if I am full of joy, people will come to me to find out what makes me so happy. If I have a life which is not filled with stress, no matter what the conditions around me are, people will want to find out why. What a beautiful opportunity to show people the *Joy of the Lord*. We never know when someone is listening or watching us, so if we are rejoicing, people will see the Christian experience as something to be desired.

Will you join us in proclaiming the joy of Jesus, to a lost and dying world, giving hope to those who have none? If you can rejoice over the love God has for you, wait until you have the chance to rejoice over someone who finds the Lord because you told him about Jesus Christ, the Savior. Or, you can keep it to yourself and you will never find out what the Lord means when He says,

"If you will proclaim me before men, I will proclaim you before my Father."

STEP FIVE
REJOICE PUBLICLY

We have become ready and willing to give our testimony for Christ Jesus - others need to hear of the wonder-working power of our God.

Rejoicing publicly seems to be something that is conspicuously missing today in our world of "easy believism." Just the other day, someone (a professing Christian by the way) said to my wife, "Do you always have to be so exuberant, it gets a little embarrassing." Imagine not wanting her to be excited about having eternal life, not to mention the joy unspeakable we have now! (I Peter 1:8).

Sounds strange? You bet it is, and that is exactly what I am talking about. I've even heard people say, "I've been really lucky, I got saved about six months ago and no one at work has found out about it yet." Statements like those can really confuse you, if you don't have a firm grasp on what you believe.

Another good one is, "Well the Lord hasn't convicted me about rejoicing publicly yet, so He must not want me to do it." There is a gigantic mistake in that kind of statement. If the Bible says to do, or not to do something, that is exactly what God wants. It would be like having an employer tell us that our work shift starts at 8:00 in the morning, and since we have been coming in at 8:30 for the last few weeks, we decide it must be OK to go on the way we were. Don't be fooled; if God said it, that ends it. A saying we can use to shore up our faith in these times is, "God said it, I believe it and that settles it!" Always remember, the Word of God is straight forward and simple to understand through prayer and continued study, combined with a good Christian Church which teaches the Word of God.

Right now would be a good time to answer some questions people ask about the subject of rejoicing publicly. If you have more questions, find another person who is interested and do some research of your own. There are ample instances of public rejoicing in the Word of God and they will help you to overcome some of your fears. Right now you might think that rejoicing publicly will be easy, but wait until you begin, your throat will more than likely dry up, your hands will be shaky and sweaty, your tongue will refuse to work and your brain will go on vacation. Don't be concerned, it is a common malady that we all learn to overcome with practice.

Don't be concerned about making mistakes, just lean on Romans 8:28,

We are assured and know that [God being a partner in their labor] all things work together and are [fitting into a plan] for good to and for those who love God and are called according to [His] design and purpose.

A teacher whom I enjoy said recently, "I'd rather have one person witnessing and making mistakes than a hundred contented Christians who never do squat."

1. Does the Bible say to rejoice publicly?

Psalm 5:11 -

But let all those who take refuge and put their trust in You rejoice; let them ever sing and shout for joy, because You make a covering over them and defend them; let those also who love Your name be joyful in You and be in high spirits.

Psalm 32:11 -

Be glad in the Lord and rejoice, you [uncompromisingly] righteous [you who are upright and in right standing with Him]; shout for joy, all you upright in heart!

Philippians 4:4 -

Rejoice in the Lord always [delight, gladden yourselves in Him];   again I say, Rejoice!

I Thessalonians 5:16 & 18 -

Be happy [in your faith] and rejoice and be glad-hearted continually (always); Thank [God] in everything [no matter what the circumstances may be, be thankful and give thanks], for this is the will of God for you [who are] in Christ Jesus [the Revealer and Mediator of that will].

WHAT IS YOUR PERSONAL RESPONSE?

_____

_____

_____

_____

_____

There are a number of reasons why we should rejoice, among them are:

• We have salvation from sure judgment and an eternity in Hell.[1]

• We have deliverance from the bondages of sin.[2]

• We are victorious since Jesus defeated Satan and the power and penalty of our sin is gone.[3]

• We have peace that passes understanding.[4]

• We are joint heirs with Christ in God's eternal kingdom.[5]

• We have finally found Someone Whom we can trust, Who will never lie to us or make excuses for not being there when we need Him![6]

These are just a few of the reasons we should rejoice publicly. You can find many more if you will look into God's Living Word. So now we know that we need to rejoice, but why publicly?

The first and most important reason is simply because the Word of God says so. When the Word tells us to do something, that is a command, not an option we can choose if we feel like it. Read Matthew 7:21 to see the consequences of not following the

Word of God. Is that a risk worth taking? The
answer to that question is simple; no risk that jeop-
ardizes your relationship with the Lord is worth
it!

The second, and just as important, reason to rejoice publicly is that we have a commission from God
to tell the world about Jesus (see Matthew 28:19 &
20). It would be a drag to see someone we knew,
standing before the judgment seat of God, saying,
"No one ever told me about Jesus;" remember again
Ezekiel 33:2-6. We will be held accountable for
every word and deed, so we need to witness to our
faith whenever we have the opportunity.

2. Why do I need to tell others of my faith?

Matthew 10:32 -

*Therefore, everyone who acknowledges Me
before men and confesses Me [out of a state of
oneness with Me], I will also acknowledge
him before My Father Who is in heaven and
confess [that I am abiding in] him.*

Romans 10:9 -

*Because if you acknowledge and confess with
your lips that Jesus is Lord and in your heart
believe (adhere to, trust in, and rely on the
truth) that God raised Him from the dead,
you will be saved.*

Romans 10:14 -

*But how are people to call upon Him Whom
they have not believed [in Whom they have no
faith, on Whom they have no reliance]? And*

how are they to believe in Him [adhere to, trust in, and rely upon Him] of Whom they have never heard? And how are they to hear without a preacher?

II Corinthians 4:1-3 -

Therefore, since we do hold and engage in this ministry by the mercy of God [granting us favor, benefits, opportunities, and especially salvation], we do not get discouraged (spiritless and despondent with fear) or become faint with weariness and exhaustion.

WHAT IS YOUR PERSONAL RESPONSE?

_____
_____
_____
_____
_____

Obviously, our willingness to share our faith with others is an important issue. Certainly, we want our names to be written in the Lamb's Book of Life.[7] The implication is that if we refuse to confess Jesus as Lord before men, He will refuse to confess our faith before the Father. In fact, the next verse says that exact thing.[8] However, the possibility of penalty should not be the prime reason for our actions. We also see that if we speak out that Jesus is Lord, we will be saved.[9] Here again, we face the possibility of gambling with eternity. Do we want to take any chances? NO! Not if we have the brains that God gave little geese.

Many of us have the wrong impression about who
is a preacher. The man at your church who teaches
out of God's Word is a pastor. Anyone who proclaims
the Gospel of Christ Jesus is a preacher, so let's get
on with our preaching. Avoid at all costs viewing the
ministry of the Gospel as a moneymaking venture.
The Word of God is a living and vital instrument of
God's will and should be handled as such. Of course,
there are many people today who misuse the Gospel
and who handle it without honesty.[10] They will be
dealt with in due time and are of no concern to us
now. Our concern is for our own walk with the Lord.
He didn't make us fruit inspectors (Galatians 5).

When we don't share our faith, we are depriving
people of what could be their last chance to make a
decision for Christ.[11] How would it be to find out
that someone to whom you had considered witnessing had died moments after you talked to them? If
they go to Hell, whose hands are bloody?

Another common concern is that we won't do it
well, so we will keep quiet until we are good at sharing. After all, no one wants to be made fun of or
laughed at. If we are Christians and don't share,
Satan is already laughing. The only way to get good
at sharing is the same way we learn to be skilled at
anything we do... **practice!!!**

3. What if they laugh or make fun of me?

I Peter 4:13 & 14 -

But insofar as you are sharing Christ's
sufferings, rejoice, so that when His glory
[full radiance and splendor] is revealed,

you may also rejoice with triumph [exultantly]. If you are censured and suffer abuse [because you bear] the name of Christ, blessed [are you - happy, fortunate, to be envied, with life-joy, and satisfaction in God's favor and salvation, regardless of your outward condition], because the Spirit of glory, the Spirit of God, is resting upon you. On their part He is blasphemed, but on your part He is glorified.

I Peter 2:20 -

[After all] what kind of glory [is there in it] if, when you do wrong and are punished for it, you take it patiently? But if you bear patiently with suffering [which results] when you do right and that is undeserved, it is acceptable and pleasing to God.

I Peter 3:17 -

For [it is] better to suffer [unjustly] for doing right, if that should be God's will, than to suffer [justly] for doing wrong.

Acts 5:41 -

So they went out from the presence of the council (Sanhedrin), rejoicing that they were being counted worthy [dignified by the indignity] to suffer shame and be exposed to disgrace for [the sake of] His name.

WHAT IS YOUR PERSONAL RESPONSE?

_____

_____

_____

_____

_____

Here we have some examples of why that type of reaction is something we can't allow to stop us from sharing. Jesus was mocked and laughed at while He was here on His earthly ministry.[12] In fact, He was treated much worse than that.[13] None of us can ever suffer as He was made to suffer.[14] However, when He comes again (which will be very soon), we will for a certainty be exceedingly glad to have suffered for Him. Imagine having someone meet you at the gates of Heaven saying, "Man, am I glad that you kept after me. If you hadn't, I'd be in Hell!"

All of us know what it is like to be made to suffer for doing wrong, even though most of us are reluctant to admit that we did wrong. When we are mocked or scorned for doing right (sharing our testimony), we should consider it as a sign that we are doing well (see Luke 6:26). When I am not meeting any opposition from the world around me, I get nervous.[15]

One thing is apparent. In this world there is going to be evil and suffering. Shouldn't we prefer to suffer for good rather than for evil? If we suffer for doing good, God will bless us for it. If we suffer for doing evil, we have earned it.[16] Of course, many of us who came from a life of compulsive behavior and wickedness feel that even if we were to try to share, no one would listen; let's look at a few examples of others who felt that they weren't right for the part either.

4. Why would anyone listen to me?

Exodus 4:1 & 10 -

And Moses answered, But behold, they will not believe me or listen to and obey my voice; for they will say, The Lord has not appeared to you. And Moses said to the Lord, O Lord, I am not eloquent or a man of words, neither before nor since You have spoken to Your servant; for I am slow of speech and have a heavy and awkward tongue.

Judges 6:15 & 16 -

Gideon said to Him, Oh Lord, how can I deliver Israel? Behold, my clan is the poorest in Manasseh, and I am the least in my father's house. The Lord said to him, Surely I will be with you, and you shall smite the Midianites as one man.

Jeremiah 1:6-8 -

Then said I, Ah, Lord God! Behold, I cannot speak, for I am only a youth. But the Lord said to me, Say not, I am only a youth; for you shall go to all to whom I shall send you, and whatever I command you, you shall speak. Be not afraid of them [their faces], for I am with you to deliver you, says the Lord.

Acts 22:19 & 20 -

And I said, Lord, they themselves well know that throughout all the synagogues I cast into prison and flogged those who believed on (adhered to and trusted in and relied on) You. And when the blood of Your witness (martyr) Stephen was shed, I also was personally standing by and consenting and approving and guarding the garments of those who slew him.

WHAT IS YOUR PERSONAL RESPONSE?

_____
_____
_____
_____
_____
_____

Wasn't Moses raised as the son of Pharaoh's daughter? Wasn't he honored in the court of the king of Egypt? Yes, he was, and with all that, you would think that he would be able to just take off, proclaiming God's message boldly. But Moses was victim of the same malady which strikes us. He, too, was a coward when it came to taking a message to people he thought didn't want to hear it. Even though Moses begged the Lord God to get someone else. God knew exactly who He wanted. He knows what He wants of us, too.

When God called Gideon to lead the army of Israel, he was the smallest and least worthy in his
father's house and his father's house was one of the
poorest in their town. How could God possibly want
someone like that when there were mighty men of
valor around? God, again, knew exactly what He
was doing. Gideon had a willing heart and wasn't
looking for personal glory. God can empower
whoever He will to do the work He has chosen for
them. Are you ready to answer the call?

Jeremiah was called when he was still very
young. This was especially difficult for him as he
lived in a society where young men had no authority.
God not only promised to be with him, but also to
deliver him from the wrath of any who opposed him.
Take comfort, Jesus Christ is the same yesterday,
and today, and forever.[17]

OK, so you aren't too old, too young, too sick, too
scared, too slow, or too weak to share the gospel.
Maybe your excuse will be one of the ones I used at
first. "I can't share the gospel. I used to beat up
Christians. I made fun of them. I ridiculed them. I
used them. They will never listen to me."

First of all, we aren't concerned about sharing
our faith with those who are already Christians.
Secondly, if God empowers you, all things are
possible through Christ Jesus who strengthens us
(see Philippians 4:13). If you still have excuses,
study God's Word a while longer and you will find
the answer to your excuse written thousands of
years ago.

I'll never forget something a man said to me a few years ago, "If you would like to see changes in your condition, get your *'BUT'* out of the way: *'I'd do it, but..., I'm too old, I'm too young, I'm too sick, I'm too busy, I'm too poor, I'm too dumb, I'm not well trained, I'm over-qualified, etc....'"* Will you get your *"but"* out of the way? Will you join us in the fight for a lost and dying world?

ADDITIONAL SCRIPTURES

1. Matthew 25:31-46
2. Romans 8:21
3. Colossians 2:15 & Revelation 1:18
4. Philippians 4:7
5. Romans 8:17
6. Hebrews 6:18 & Hebrews 13:5
7. Revelation 21:27
8. Matthew 10:33
9. Romans 10:9
10. Colossians 2:8
11. II Corinthians 4:3
12. Matthew 27:29
13. John 19:1-3
14. John 19:23
15. James 4:4
16. I Peter 2:20
17. Hebrews 13:8

STEP SIX

It soon was clear to me that forming Christian relationships and friendships was the only way that I would have any friends, as the people who knew Linda and me before we were saved either tried to get us to party or didn't want to talk to us anymore. I guess they didn't want to continually talk about the Lord and that was all that I was interested in; that hasn't changed to this day. The old friends Linda and I had were still doing the same things which we used to do. The only logical step we saw was to find new ones. After all, if we were still going to hang around with the same people and do the same things, why would the outcome be any different? Doing the things they did, and having the attitudes they had, brought me to my near-fatal condition. After all, haven't you noticed that we all have a tendency to act like those with whom we associate?

When you are bound by compulsive behavior as I was, you have to develop completely new habits and associations. What lasting good would this "New Life" have been if I had gone right back to the same old stuff and the same old habits that were destroying me in the first place? We noticed that those who were among our old friends who didn't know the

Lord, were most likely to be the ones who would try to tear down our new faith. Of course, they thought that they were helping us by not letting us get sucked into some cult; I don't think they intentionally set out to harm us.

Think of sometime in your life when you started to go a different direction than the one your friends were taking; people are always afraid of the unknown and that fear can be destructive and dangerous. The reason for this behavior is that light has no fellowship with darkness (II Corinthians 6:14).

Others of our "friends" did willfully attempt to lure us back into the sins we had left behind. I remember playing golf with a friend of mine shortly after we were saved. It was an ordeal I'll never forget. Usually playing golf is a pleasant, enjoyable time for me, but this time it was something else. From the moment I picked him up at his house he constantly tried, by every method he could conceive, to get me to have a beer, have a little coke (cocaine) or have a shooter of whiskey. No matter what I said, he would not relent. I thought I would never see the 18th hole and be done with him. When it was all over and I had dropped my "friend" off, a sense of relief came over me that was like a breath of fresh air; I remember praising God all the way home and being excited by the power of His love in keeping me from giving in. I know that I never would have resisted if I had been on my own.

Jealousy is the root of this kind of attitude and some of your "friends" will react the same way.

When they see that you have something that they don't have, they will usually try to ruin it for you. It is always easier (in their mind) for them to drag you back to their level, than to expend the effort to find out if what you have is for real.

After that day I was, and continue to be, careful who I am around when I am trying to relax or just have fun. The next time I went to the golf course, I went with a Christian friend of mine and had a wonderful time. We spent six hours talking about God's Word, His Son, and discussing areas of our lives which we felt were still weak. Many times we can benefit greatly from the advice and counsel of a more mature Christian friend. Their advice is given to help you grow rather than to bring you down to a lower level.

Linda and I didn't stop sharing our faith with people who don't know the Lord, we just became careful who we called our friends. Real friends are people you can bare your soul to, and people you can confess the darkest secrets of your heart without fear of reprisal or gossip. For the first time in my life, I was beginning to find people I could be open with and not feel used or abused. What an experience! After over thirty years of not trusting or opening up to anyone, I found that in the family of God there were some friends for me; this is not to say that everyone who says that they are a "Christian" can automatically be trusted. Rather it means that when you find someone with whom your new spirit bears witness, you have a friend no matter what happens.

Our new friends were the ones who helped us to form our habits of regular worship, Sunday School, Bible study, consistent prayer, and witnessing to a lost and dying world. Our old friends certainly wouldn't have encouraged any of that!

About this time Linda, found herself in a situation which caused her to change employers. The job she had when we were saved paid her about $45,000 a year with a car (a BMW), and full medical benefits. Shortly after we were saved, she became convinced that some of the practices required of her were unacceptable for our new walk with the Lord. We went to our close friend and spiritual counsellor, John Rutherford, for advice since we felt that he would give us good counsel. It was good and sound, but hard to swallow.

After listening to the problem and praying with us, John simply said, "Linda, you'll have to quit that job." What did we do? We decided that our answer from John and from the Lord in prayer were the same, so Linda quit that job and we trusted the consequences to God. The good news is that He (Jesus) is worthy of that trust and has never slackened in His care of Linda and me, or our children. It was a big step, but the question we had to answer was, "Who do you fear?" (Matthew 10:28). We cast our cares on Him and He takes care of us (I Peter 5:7).

We have, over the last few years, made some lifelong friends, both with people who were already Christians and with people who met the Living Lord through our ministry. These friends are a comfort to us both in hard times and in times of rejoicing.

Having someone who knows you as you really are, and loves you anyway is always a joy. We are never alone anymore. Our Lord Jesus will never leave us or forsake us (Hebrews 13:5). Our friends will love us, in spite of ourselves.

Having friends who love us enough to rebuke and reprove us, is a blessing that doesn't exist outside of the family of God. Only those who truly love us and care for us will have the courage to do that. Anyone can tell us how wonderful we are when we do good. Friends will rescue us when we are stumbling or taking a wrong path. Praise God, "His Mercy endureth forever" (Psalm 136:1-26).

Will you start today, will you give up your past and begin your walk into a "New Life" with the Lord Jesus as your constant companion and ever present champion in whatever circumstances you may find yourself? If there is someone, or something else in the world that never fails, I certainly never found it, and I had many years of futile searching. Do yourself a favor, try God's way first, and if it doesn't work (which it will), then fail your own way!

STEP SIX

FORM CHRISTIAN FRIENDSHIPS AND RELATIONSHIPS

We became aware that the three greatest enemies of our New Life were old places, old friends and old habits. We desire to remain free!

Through our involvement in New Life Ministries, we have seen many instances which confirm this need for freedom from compulsive behavior. Some people who started out strong for the Lord, fell away because they refused to give up old friends, old habits and old places. Those three are our greatest enemies in terms of lasting change in our lives.

We also have seen God work in the lives of people when everyone said, "Don't bother, they're not worth the effort." Some of them had made quite a few tries at living right, only to fail. When they were willing to try this step, suddenly they were able to make it.

Another benefit of this step is found in our ability to learn to resist temptation. Just being away from temptation on a regular basis, even for a few hours a day, will enable you to discern more clearly how to avoid even the presence of temptation. When we are around people who are not involved in lifestyle sin, we are given a time of rest from temptation and a chance to learn new activities. You'd be surprised how much fun you can have with a group of people who don't do things which the world says are fun, but which are called sin in God's Word.

A good example of the problem created by old places, old habits and old friends, is that we tend to mirror those we associate with. I know, you'll say "Well, other people might, but not me;" however, you do become like the people around you, no matter how much you care to deny it! Let me give you an example. Have you noticed that when you are around someone with a southern accent for a while, you start to use some of their speech mannerisms? If you

are around a person who is into flying, you find yourself being interested in it, too. If you are around
someone who is into astrology or other mystical
practices, do you start being interested? Of course
you do; that is exactly my point. The profundity
our mothers taught us, "You're known by the
company you keep," is true.

As Linda and I began to study God's Word
and to develop our prayer life, we found many
confirmations of this concept. Being separate
was a lifesaver for us. We had to exercise caution not to isolate ourselves though; that too,
would have been wrong. We are told by our
Savior not to hide our light (Matthew 5:15 & 16)
and that we, through sharing, may save many
from an eternity of torment.

Looking back to the last few days before we were
"born again," we will be eternally grateful to a man
named Ted Schultz. If he had decided not to reach
out to us in a public restaurant, we might never have
been saved. He is one of my best friends and he
probably doesn't know it, since we have lost
track of him.

Our natural tendency to talk about what we were
excited about was another good reason for finding
new friends and relationships. With our Christian
friends we could discuss scriptures, ask questions,
form our system of beliefs and pray together. We
discovered as an added benefit that Christians have
fun, too. Our impression that Christians don't have
any fun because of all of the rules they have to live
by, was another lie from Satan to keep us away from

wanting to know the Living Lord. Religion is where rules are, not in scriptural Christianity. Remember, our freedom is the freedom not to do the things which we don't want to do.

That freedom is enhanced by Christian friends. They can be a real boon in times of tribulation and a real blessing in times of abundance.

1. Why can't I keep my old friends?

Proverbs 4:14 & 15 -

Enter not into the path of the wicked, and go not in the way of evil men. Avoid it, do not go on it; turn from it and pass on.

Proverbs 13:20 -

He who walks [as a companion] with wise men is wise, but he who associates with [self-confident] fools is [a fool himself and] shall smart for it.

Joshua 23:11-13 -

Be very watchful of yourselves, therefore, to love the Lord your God. For if you turn back and adhere to the remnant of these nations left among you and make marriages with them, you marrying their women and they yours, Know with certainty that the Lord your God will not continue to drive these nations from before you; but they shall be a snare and trap to you, and a scourge in your sides and thorns in your eyes, until you perish from off this good land which the Lord your God has given you.

I Corinthians 15:33 & 34 -

Do not be so deceived and misled! Evil companionships (communion, associations) corrupt and deprave good manners and morals and character. Awake [from your drunken stupor and return] to sober sense and your right minds, and sin no more. For some of you have not the knowledge of God [you are utterly and willfully and disgracefully ignorant, and continue to be so, lacking the sense of God's presence and all true knowledge of Him]. I say this to your shame.

WHAT IS YOUR PERSONAL RESPONSE?

_____
_____
_____
_____
_____
_____

This is a commonly asked question and the biblical answers are very clear. We have just looked at four, but there are many more if you care to look for them. If we keep our old friends, we are entering into the path of evil, because the natural heart of man is constantly set to do evil.[1] Our old friends may have good motives, but the fact is that they fit that description unless and until they receive the Spirit of God.

With the evidence we now have, we should believe the wisdom of accepting Christ Jesus as

our Lord and Savior. God has been clear in
what He will do if we, "Come out from among
them".[2] The implication is that if we do as He
says, we will find joy and He will watch
over us, protect us, guide us and constantly be
with us![3]

The final reference we just used is a two part message for us. We are told not to be tricked, companionship with sinners will ruin our Christian
walk, and we are told to awake to righteousness. In awakening to righteousness, we are
reminded again that we are to share our faith
with the people around us and if we don't, it
will be for our shame.[4]

You may say, "That's fine, but all you have done is
imply that I should make new friends." Fair enough,
let's find some examples of sinners and confessing
Christians whom we are to avoid.

**2. Does the Bible say to find new friends and
relationships?**

I Corinthians 5:11 -

*But now I write to you not to associate with
anyone who bears the name of [Christian]
brother if he is known to be guilty of immorality or greed, or is an idolater [whose
soul is devoted to any object that usurps the
place of God], or is a person with a foul
tongue [railing, abusing, reviling, slander-
ing], or is a drunkard or a swindler or a rob-
ber. [No] you must not so much as eat with
such a person.*

II Thessalonians 3:6 -

Now we charge you, brethren, in the name and on the authority of our Lord Jesus Christ (the Messiah) that you withdraw and keep away from every brother (fellow believer) who is slack in the performance of duty and is disorderly, living as a shirker and not walking in accord with the traditions and instructions that you have received from us.

II Corinthians 6:14 -

Do not be unequally yoked with unbelievers [do not make mismated alliances with them or come under a different yoke with them, inconsistent with your faith]. For what partnership have right living and right standing with God with iniquity and lawlessness? Or how can light have fellowship with darkness?

II Corinthians 6:17 -

So, come out from among [unbelievers], and separate (sever) yourselves from them, says the Lord, and touch not [any] unclean thing; then I will receive you kindly and treat you with favor.

Hebrews 10:25 -

Not forsaking or neglecting to assemble together [as believers], as is the habit of some people, but admonishing (warning, urging, and encouraging) one another, and all the more faithfully as you see the day approaching.

WHAT IS YOUR PERSONAL RESPONSE?

_____

_____

_____

_____

_____

_____

The first two scriptures we just looked at deal with what is called a carnal or back-slidden Christian. If you have had only limited experience with Christians, you may think that we don't act like these scriptures describe. Unfortunately, we sometimes do. You see Christians are human beings, and as such, are prone to falling victim to their fleshly lusts.[5] If you stick around long enough, you will meet people like this inside the group who profess to be Christians. When you do meet someone like this, stay away from them, don't listen to them, literally have nothing to do with them.[6] After you have grown past the spiritual infant stage, you will be taught by the Word of God how to deal with and how to minister to this group of people.

The next group we deal with is nonbelievers. Being unequally yoked with them can mean everything from marriage to business dealings.[7] This does not mean that when you get saved if your husband or wife doesn't accept Christ immediately, you can divorce them. Nor does it mean that you should quit your job because there are unsaved people there.

What it does mean is, after you are saved, don't marry an unsaved person, and don't go into business with unsaved people. In fact, it would be wise to avoid those same alliances with Christians who are living in sin.

Those two examples aren't the full extent of the phrase, "unequally yoked." Your friends, associates, places to go, and things to do should also be considered. In II Corinthians 6:14 & 17, we see that our spiritual health may indeed depend upon our obeying this command of our Lord. Study Proverbs 24:1-3 very carefully; in fact, committing it to memory would be a good idea. If you keep what He says in mind, you will avoid a lot of unnecessary pain. It should also be comforting to know that forming these new friendships and relationships will help us continue to walk upright in the eyes of God. In fact, if the desire of our hearts is to completely follow His commands, we will find the joy of the Lord always with us.[8]

"Not forsaking the fellowship of believers" is also a good method of ensuring that our walk with Jesus is growing and we are not slipping back into sin. Notice that we are told to "warn, urge and encourage each other" when we see someone in a potential problem. Again, we see scriptural proof that our friends and associates will have a tremendous impact for good or evil in our lives. The choice is yours, will you choose Christian friends and associates or will you give in to Satan and be once again trapped in his snares?[9]

3. Will new friends and relationships help keep me free?

Psalm 1:1 -

Blessed (happy, fortunate, prosperous, and enviable) is the man who walks and lives not in the counsel of the ungodly [following their advice, their plans and purposes], nor stands [submissive and inactive] in the path where sinners walk, nor sits down [to relax and rest] where the scornful [and the mockers] gather.

Luke 10:1 -

Now after this the Lord chose and appointed seventy others and sent them out ahead of Him, two by two, into every town and place where He Himself was about to come (visit).

I Thessalonians 5:11 -

Therefore encourage (admonish, exhort) one another and edify (strengthen and build up) one another, just as you are doing.

Ecclesiastes 4:9-12 -

Two are better than one, because they have a good [more satisfying] reward for their labor; For if they fall, the one will lift up his fellow. But woe to him who is alone when he falls and has not another to lift him up! Again, if two lie down together, then they have warmth; but how can one be warm alone? And though a man might prevail against him who is alone, two will withstand him. A threefold cord is not quickly broken.

WHAT IS YOUR PERSONAL RESPONSE?

_____

_____

_____

_____

_____

We find in these scriptures a number of good reasons how our new friends and relationships will help us to stay free of our previous bondages. If we are spending our "A" time with other Christians, we are decreasing the risk of having the counsel of the ungodly and we are not in the midst of the sin of sinners.[10]

Avoiding our tendency to be judgmental and scornful is something that we will have to work on until the Lord comes again. That part of us dies very hard; "Judge not lest ye be not judged;"[11] "He who judges without mercy will be judged without mercy."[12] The Lord has told us that we need to learn that truth, but we have a hard time accepting it. Here is where our new friends will be of great help. We can agree to watch each other and help each other stop as soon as we start falling back into the old ways.[13]

A lot of people don't know what the word "edify" means. For those of you who don't, here is a simple definition: To instruct or improve, to build up and to perfect (the process, not the end result). One of the chief advantages of Christian friends and associates

is that we can be mutually beneficial and instruc-
tive. When Jesus sent the disciples out two by two,
He was following a principle given to us by a man
who is said to be the wisest man who ever lived.
Solomon tells us why two are better than one and he
says that three are even better. I'd imagine that you
can think of numerous times in your life when two or
three would have saved your bacon! I know that
I can think of a couple of times in the ministry,
when I could have saved myself a massive
amount of discomfort if I had remembered what
Solomon and Jesus said.

Now that we have that settled, some of you are
probably saying to yourselves, "I can overcome all of
this without Christian friends and associates. I'll
give up my old ones and go it alone." Don't be
stupid, you will only fail again. The Bible is
very clear about that. Let's look at what the
Word says.

**4. How will friends help me to resist tempta-
tion?**

Ecclesiastes 8:11 -

*Because the sentence against an evil work is
not executed speedily, the hearts of the sons of
men are fully set to do evil.*

Galatians 6:1 & 2 -

*Brethren, if any person is overtaken in mis-
conduct or sin of any sort, you who are
spiritual [who are responsive to and controlled by the Spirit] should set him right and restore and reinstate him, without any sense of*

superiority and with all gentleness, keeping an attentive eye on yourself, lest you should be tempted also. Bear (endure, carry) one another's burdens and troublesome moral faults, and in this way fulfill and observe perfectly the law of Christ (the Messiah) and complete what is lacking [in your obedience to it].

Romans 7:18 & 19 -

For I know that nothing good dwells within me, that is, in my flesh. I can will what is right, but I cannot perform it. [I have the intention and urge to do what is right, but no power to carry it out.]

Proverbs 17:17 -

A friend loves at all times, and is born, as is a brother, for adversity.

WHAT IS YOUR PERSONAL RESPONSE?

_____
_____
_____
_____
_____
_____

Several times over the last few years, we have seen people (who were just beginning to get their lives back together) crash and burn over the very truism that is stated in Ecclesiastes 8:11. They have been delivered from their bondage to sin and saved

from a life of misery and torment only to return
to their own folly. We don't know the mind of
God, so we don't know why evil is not instantly
punished.[15]

The fact that it is not is evident in the world
around us. However, because it isn't, we hear statements like, "Well I've been doing this for a while now
and God hasn't punished me yet." The wording of the
excuse changes, but the underlying problem hasn't.
Even after we are born again, we have our carnal nature to deal with.[16]

With practice, our ability to resist self becomes
easier but the battle never stops. We seem to want
to trade one set of problems for another. On our own,
we feel like Paul in the seventh chapter of the book
of Romans. When we have Christian friends our
ability to resist is enhanced by the principle stated
in Ecclesiastes 4:9-12. Even when we aren't capable
of doing the right thing, we can stop our mistakes
and go to our friends for help. We can pray together,
talk together, confess our weaknesses to each other,
and get the counsel of more mature Christians about
our daily problems.[17]

This is sometimes difficult as we often feel that
needing help is a sign of weakness. Actually, the
truth is that it takes real courage to admit our
shortcomings to someone else. We are afraid they
will repeat it or they will scorn us and reject us. If
you have real Christian friends, you will not have to
worry about those things. Take care, however, that
you follow Paul's advice in I Timothy 5:22. His advice is to his disciple who was starting out in

ministry, but it applies to us also in regard to where we place our trust. Just because someone says he is a Christian, doesn't mean he is any more than if someone claims their check is in the mail, it has actually been sent. We are taught by the Word of God to test all spirits.[18] So we should exercise caution about telling our innermost secrets.

We are admonished to help a brother caught up in a sin, not shoot him.[19] One of the biggest problems we have today in the Church is that we often shoot our wounded. Let's remember where we came from and have compassion on a brother or sister in need.[20] We may find ourselves in need in the future, so why bring on more suffering?[21]

Covering a transgression (sin) is the act of helping and protecting a brother or sister until they are on their feet again. Are we willing to do that?[22]

Never, I repeat, never, allow yourself to get so good in your own sight that the sight of your fellow Christian in trouble doesn't cause your heart to have pain and fear for them. Be ready to help and to comfort those in need both inside of the Body of Christ and outside.

Now that you will be looking for new friends who will be real friends, work on becoming the kind of friend that you will be seeking. Does that sound like the "Golden Rule"? It should. That is exactly the idea we are trying to convey. The Word of God is full of this meaning. Will you listen to wise counsel or will you be like the person who is spoken of in Proverbs 17:12 & 24?

ADDITIONAL SCRIPTURES

1. Genesis 6:5
2. II Corinthians 6:17
3. Isaiah 52:12 and Matthew 28:20
4. I Corinthians 15:33 & 34
5. Romans 7:18-19
6. I Corinthians 5:11
7. II Corinthians 6:14
8. Matthew 25:21
9. II Peter 3:17
10. Psalm 1:1
11. Matthew 7:1
12. Matthew 7:2
13. Ephesians 4:25-32
14. Ecclesiastes 4:9-12
15. Ecclesiastes 8:11
16. Romans 7:23
17. Proverbs 11:14
18. I John 4:1
19. Galatians 6:1 & 2
20. Ephesians 4:32
21. Galatians 6:2
22. Proverbs 17:9 & 17

STEP SEVEN

It seems that a hunger for God's word comes at different times in different lives. The day Linda and I were saved, I immediately began to devour God's word. Linda, however, didn't develop this intense hunger for the Word for a few months. The same day that we got saved, I went to Michele's house (my sister) and found a Bible which was left there by her daughter, Beverly. Although at that time, neither Michele nor Beverly were Christians, the Bible was there and my sister said I could have it.

Since I had promised to believe, trust, and obey the Lord, I knew that I had to read the Bible; I began reading in Genesis and every spare moment of the day and night was spent reading the Bible until I finished Revelation. I still have that Bible although it is a version that I don't especially care for now. It still holds a special place in my heart. There are, I am sure, a lot of well-meaning Christians who would find fault with that particular version (the Living Bible), but it was written in English which I could readily understand. Although I am not particularly fond of that version now, it was a good place to start.

It seemed that I couldn't get enough of the Word, or learn enough about the Kingdom of God. The

more I read, the more I found it to be compelling. I
had books from over the years of my life which I really enjoyed, but never had I found one that I wanted
to read again and again. Every time I read the scriptures, some new information or knowledge is there
waiting for me. The Bible constantly causes me to
think and challenges me to study more and more
deeply into God's precepts. Praise God, the Bible
doesn't grow old or stale. It is never predictable or
pat. After repeated readings and concentrated
studies, I can truthfully say that, for me, it is unquestionably the inspired Living Word of God. That
is the only plausible explanation for its newness and
ageless applicability.

Where else can someone with no formal training
find a guide for every step of his or her life, no matter where or when they live? I have found, without
exception, that anyone who is "born again," can understand God's Word if they truly desire to know
Him and are not just looking for an easy way around
some difficulty in their lives.

It should be noted, at this point, that Linda may
not have developed a burning desire for studying the
Word as soon as I did, but she began a daily habit of
Bible study right away. She didn't just sit and wait
for God to infuse her with the desire for intense
study. That would make about as much sense as
going to college and waiting to be inspired to study.
When you begin, you study until the fire of desire for
knowledge comes, and it will. I know other people
who were in the family of God for years before they
experienced this burning desire to draw nearer to

the Lord. He, in His timing, knows the right time for each of us and He will prompt us. His Word however, does exhort, command and encourage regular Bible study. If the Word says to study, that is all the prompting we should need.

Change is never easy and growth involves a certain amount of pain, but the question you should be asking yourself is, "Will it be worth it?" Consider that the Promise of God is eternal life in the Presence of the Living Lord, and you can only reach one logical answer. YES, IT WILL! Breaking old habits is hard work, and forming new ones is an effort, but if it were easy, would it be worth anything? We all know that making bad habits is the easiest thing in the world; the best time to start building good habits is now.

I can think of no better way to learn of our Heavenly Father than in His Word. There we will find His character, personality, and His person waiting for our lives to come into fellowship with Him. Through the study of His Word, the Lord continually shows Linda and me areas of our lives which need His touch, and areas of need in others' lives where we can minister.

As we continue to study and learn, He also displays His majesty and mercy in areas where we never expect to find them. As His will for us is revealed in His Word, our lives take on more and more excitement and hope than we could have ever dreamed possible. As with any other learning process, learning God's will and doing it will involve making mistakes; not His, but ours. The good news

we discover in our learning is that even when we
blow it, He is faithful and never leaves us in the
midst of our disasters. Like a loving father, which
He is, He is there to pick us up when we stumble and
to dust us off, encourage us to continue, and help us
on our way!

In His Word, the Lord will show you exactly what
you need for every situation you may come against.
We could search for hours for the appropriate scripture each time we are in a crisis. However, I'm referring to something more than that; if you have a
consistent continuous habit of daily Bible study, you
will find, in the majority of cases, the decisions
which you make will be the proper ones. He has told
us to hide His Word in our hearts, and I don't know
of any other way to do that except to study it. Listening to some minister's teaching is good, but will
not take the place of YOU learning the Word of God
for yourself. Start developing a habit of Bible study
and you, too, will find that even when you are wrong,
He is still the Loving Father. Praise God, "His mercy
endureth forever."

STEP SEVEN
STUDY GOD'S WORD

**We have realized that the Bible is the
inspired Word of God, we are developing a daily habit of Bible study - it is
what God says that counts; we will find
Him in His Word!**

The Word of God has the power and authority to mold us and to shape us into the type of beings we were originally created to be. In the Word, we will also discover His Son, and His Spirit. The Three Persons of the Trinity make up the divine Godhead, and they hold redemption in Their hand for whoever will believe in Them.

In the pages of the Bible, we are shown how to gain an eternal life with God, and how to live in this one. When a person develops a habit of daily Bible study, missing that period of time studying even for one day, causes us to notice the difference and we will remember to take the time to study. Naturally, all of the Bible isn't necessarily exciting reading, but under the prompting of the Spirit of God, we will find it enlightening and enriching to our daily existence.

If a man owned a business, he would naturally reduce a large amount of the details of running his business to writing. This would ease the smooth flow of operation and the dissemination of information. He would expect his employees to follow his instructions and to be faithful to the precepts which he laid out. Can you imagine working for that man and deciding that you didn't need to know what he expected from you to keep your job? Can you imagine reading some of his instructions once in a while, if you felt like it, and expect to be able to be competent in your performance? Can you imagine that you could follow your boss' will if you only listened to your supervisors once in a while at a policy meeting, as that supervisor went over selected areas of the company policy? Sounds ridiculous? It is, and yet that's what some Christians try to do.

If we don't develop good habits of studying God's will and His Word now, when will we? I encourage you to begin today. You are the only one who can control when you will study. It will take determination and perseverance to form this habit, but it will be well worth it and you will benefit from it all your life! Set aside a specific time each day to read at least one chapter in a systematic study of God's Word. Don't just read the Bible wherever it happens to fall open; this will not give you any consistent learning.

Whenever you find areas which really minister to your heart, study it in detail and memorize it if you can. Make it a part of your life, but don't let that interrupt your daily study. Use extra time for your intensive study. Many feel that there is not enough time to do this, but let me encourage you that there is nothing more important in your life than the will and Word of God! We all have the same amount of time in the day, the difference is that some can prioritize their time more effectively than others. The Bible says that whoever we are bound to, that one will we serve. What will it be? Will you learn to serve and reverence God or will you continue serving and reverencing the ruler of this world?

1. Why is Bible study so important?

John 5:39 -

You search and investigate and pore over the Scriptures diligently, because you suppose and trust that you have eternal life through them. And these [very Scriptures] testify about Me!

John 20:31 -

But these are written (recorded) in order that you may believe that Jesus is the Christ (the Anointed One), the Son of God, and that through believing and cleaving to and trusting and relying upon Him you may have life through (in) His name [through Who He is].

Isaiah 33:6 -

And there shall be stability in your times, an abundance of salvation, wisdom and knowledge; the reverent fear and worship of the Lord is your treasure and His.

James 1:25 -

But he who looks carefully into the faultless law, the [law] of liberty, and is faithful to it and perseveres in looking into it, being not a heedless listener who forgets but an active doer [who obeys], he shall be blessed in his doing (his life of obedience).

I John 5:13 -

I write this to you who believe in (adhere to, trust in, and rely on) the name of the Son of God [in the peculiar services and blessings conferred by Him on men], so that you may know [with settled and absolute knowledge] that you [already] have life, yes, eternal life.

WHAT IS YOUR PERSONAL RESPONSE?

_____

_____

_____

_____

_____

_____

Again and again, we are told in the scriptures that God has certain and manifold
promises for us, among them the promise of
eternal life.[1] How can we grow in those promises
if we do not know them and how can we know
them in their fullness without study? As we go
on with our lives, after our conversion into the
Family of God, we require stability and strength[2]
as well as knowledge and the discernment of the
truth.[3] The Bible is our source of these re-
quirements and the source of our knowledge of
the Will of God for our lives.

Some new Christians have wondered why we
need to fear God; this fear is a reverential fear, not a
fear of destruction.[4] We will be talking of freedom
and liberty quite a bit in the following steps and you
should understand that what we will be talking
about is not license. The freedom we desire is the
freedom not to do the things which are destroying us
and that we cannot control.

In the Bible, we will learn of God's perfect law of
liberty,[5] but just knowing about it is useless. We
must learn to live in it. The Bible will also teach us

how to carry out the work and how to live for Him. Do not be deceived by any false teachers.[6] Eternal life is only given to those who believe in the Son of God, and to those who believe in His Name.[7]

There are many today who will try to deceive you by clever words and phrases but in the final analysis they deny the deity of Christ Jesus. From these teachers you will receive only confusion and lies. Avoid them like the serpents they are.

Only through Bible study will you grow in faith and assurance of your salvation. The Sword of the Spirit is our weapon against the Prince of the Power of the Air;[8] without God's Word we would be devoured by him.[9] Will you study and grow or will you be a sluggard and be torn asunder by the Adversary?

2. Will Bible study strengthen my faith?

Psalm 119:41 & 45 -

Let your mercy and loving kindness come also to me, O Lord, even Your salvation according to Your promise; And I will walk at liberty and at ease, for I have sought and inquired for [and desperately required] Your precepts.

Romans 15:4 -

For whatever was thus written in former days was written for our instruction, that by [our steadfast and patient] endurance and the encouragement [drawn] from the Scriptures we might hold fast to and cherish hope.

I Thessalonions 1:5 -

For our [preaching of the] glad tidings (the Gospel) came to you not only in word, but also in [its own inherent] power and in the Holy Spirit and with great conviction and absolute certainty [on our part]. You know what kind of men we proved [ourselves] to be among you for your good.

Matthew 4:4 -

But He replied, It has been written, Man shall not live and be upheld and sustained by bread alone, but by every word that comes forth from the mouth of God.

WHAT IS YOUR PERSONAL RESPONSE?

_____

_____

_____

_____

_____

_____

In times of testing and tribulation, we need God's strength all the more, and His strength is found in the Bible. We can study about people of God who came before us who also experienced similar trials. His mercy is always there for us, even when we are not in His perfect will. If we are assured of our salvation unto eternal life, we can indeed walk in true liberty and peace.[10] When we seek the wisdom of God before all else, all we need will be added to us.[11]

Because of the ageless truth of the scriptures, all things which were written in them, are for our learning even today! We will find by living our "new life" that the Word of God will comfort us and teach us no matter what the world does and says. As an author once wrote, "The dogs bark, but the caravan moves on."

The Word of God is our shield and our protection.[12] Earlier we mentioned the *Power and Authority* of the scriptures. Here that is confirmed. Jesus sent the Comforter to us when He departed into heaven.[13] The Holy Spirit is the power and assurance we seek and the truth in our lives, now and forever! The statement made by Jesus, in Matthew 4:4 might seem a bit obscure at first glance. However, the meaning becomes clear with a little thought and prayer. If our spiritual food is *"every word which proceedeth out of the mouth of God"* (the Bible), we will learn and continue to walk upright in God's kingdom and will be in the midst of all of His many promises (Philippians 4:1-23). Since we have chosen to be followers of Christ, doesn't it make sense to seek Him and seek the Father's Will in all things?[14] How else will we do it but by Bible study and prayer?

3. Will the Bible teach me how to live?

Psalm 119:105 -

Your word is a lamp to my feet and a light to my path.

Psalm 19:8 -

*The precepts of the Lord are right, rejoic-
ing the heart; the commandment of the
Lord is pure and bright, enlightening the
eyes.*

Proverbs 6:23 -

*For the commandment is a lamp, and the
whole teaching [of the law] is light, and
reproofs of discipline are the way of life.*

I Peter 2:1-3 -

*So be done with every trace of wickedness
(depravity, malignity) and all deceit and in-
sincerity (pretense, hypocrisy) and grudges
(envy, jealousy) and slander and evil speaking of every kind. Like newborn babies you
should crave (thirst for, earnestly desire) the
pure (unadulterated) spiritual milk, that by it
you may be nurtured and grow unto [com-
pleted] salvation, Since you have [already]
tasted the goodness and kindness of the Lord.*

Colossians 3:16 -

*Let the word [spoken by] Christ (the Messiah)
have its home [in your hearts and minds] and
dwell in you in [all its] richness, as you teach
and admonish and train one another in all
insight and intelligence and wisdom [in
spiritual things, and as you sing] psalms
and hymns and spiritual songs, making
melody to God with [His] grace in your
hearts.*

In 1967, prior to serving with the army in Viet Nam, Michael was sent to the second infantry division in Korea. He was stationed 2-1/2 miles south of the DMZ at Camp Reddick. At night they set up ambush positions along the DMZ to prevent North Korean infiltrators from crossing the U.N. sector. During daytime patrols called Hunter/Killers they searched the DMZ and shot anyone not wearing a U.S. Army uniform.

For ten months, Camp Reddick was "home" to Michael. Having never felt like he "belonged," the availability of drugs opened a door for Michael. Alcohol and drugs were readily available in the villages south of the Injin River. Some soldiers used them to forget their precarious position.

Returning from a three day tour of duty at the guard post on Hill Charlie (where they used the same trenches and bunkers left from the Korean War), Michael's squad shows the fatigue from constantly watching the North Korean troop movement along the military demarcation line.

▶ D u b b i n g themselves "The Grim Reapers," the soldiers went about their regular patrol duty knowing there was no "victory" and no "defeat." Their fight wasn't to take ground or protect their families, it was to hold a political line drawn on a faraway map.

◀ Without an identifiable "cause" for which to fight, the men had their biggest battles with themselves. Every personal problem Michael took with him to Korea was exaggerated by the situation. He was considered to be a "problem" and "unstable."

In spite of his substance abuse and his shaky record, Michael was assigned duty as an MP for the last three months of his tour of duty. This picture, taken before leaving Camp Reddick shows "Liberty Village," a Korean village built in the middle of the DMZ.

◀ After army duty was over, Michael settled down in Spokane, Washington in 1972. He went to work as a life insurance salesman. His drive brought him recognition after only six months because he sold enough insurance to be made a member of the "President's Club." It was here he met Linda, who worked in the same building for a CPA.

▶ He and Linda were married before the end of 1973 by a judge. At this time, there were signs of Michael's compulsive behavior, but the extent of it remained concealed.

▲ Since Michael's birthday and their first anniversary came on the same day, Linda spent their anniversary without Michael. The birthday celebration of the club was not suitable for wives to attend.

▲ The insignia of the "Ghost Riders" was the Iron Cross and the skull, displayed here as a decoration on Michael's birthday cake. The "Ghost Riders" had forged an alliance with the Hell's Angels for reciprocal freedom in each others' territories. That treaty did not extend to other clubs.

▶ Michael's "friends" included "Horrible Hannis," who got his name by running his motorcycle through a barbed wire fence.

◀ Michael and Linda worked on and invested in his motorcycle until he won first prize at an Auto and Boat Show. He had made his "Death Dealer" more spectacular than the bikes from the movie "Easy Rider" which were also entered in the show. Many of the features were things Michael had designed himself.

▲ As far as the eye could see ahead of Michael and Linda and behind them, motorcyclists rode from Elkhorn Park to Salem, Oregon to protest a law requiring helmets. At this time, they lived in Portland, OR.

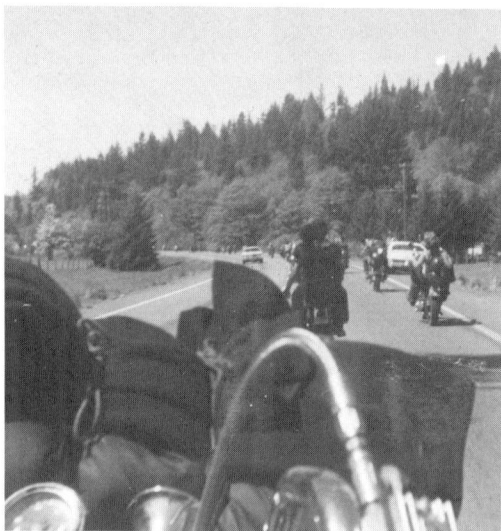

▶ Fifteen hundred motorcycles were in the "Protest Ride" - three thousand people. Their presence was felt to the extent that the law requiring helmets was repealed. The choice was left up to the riders.

▶ In 1976, Michael displayed his prize-winning motorcycle, but he didn't win again. He and Linda roamed over the Northwest on the "Death Dealer."

◀ "The biker's salute" is always given with the left hand since the right hand never leaves the throttle.

▶ In 1976, they mounted their motorcycle again to attend another "biker's rally."

◀ By 1980, Michael and Linda owned a tavern in Portland which they called "Fat Freddy's." Their logic was that since Michael spent all of his time in bars anyway, they should make it pay. Here Linda cuts her thirtieth birthday cake.

▶ The "Outsiders' Club" gathered at McGyver Park for a Spring Rally. Six to seven hundred bikers met there that day.

◀ The sky was grey with ash from the eruption of Mt. St. Helens. None of them knew what had happened until they had the taste of ash in their mouths.

◀ In 1984, Michael and Linda gave their testimony at a meeting with some of their friends who were instrumental in leading them to Christ. Left to Right are Michael, Linda, Donna and Terry Gallian. Michael and Linda even named their youngest son after Terry.

▶ Their first move was to Eastern Washington to plant a New Life Fellowship. They contacted old friends in Washington and some found Jesus, but they wanted a wider area of service so they moved back to California and worked in a mission to help others break the chains of compulsive behavior. The man pictured on this flyer had been "drunk for forty years" but his life changed as God used Michael to show him God's love.

GLORY BOUND STREET MINISTRY SACRAMENTO

JOHN 8:32   GAL 5:1   LUKE 4:18-19

◀ At "Glory Bound," Michael studied the Bible and learned to preach and minister to "misfits." The Sacramento newspaper published the following:

"Bringing people off the street, giving them a sermon and a hot meal and little bit of companionship, is a mission the Johnsons and Loureys have chosen, they said.

"'If I weren't doing this, I'd be miserable,' said Lourey, who also preaches at the Union Gospel Mission and Salvation Army in Sacramento. 'I wouldn't want to do anything else.'

"Lourey, who has been preaching at Glory Bound for the past few months, described it as a church for the people who don't fit in with the rest of society. 'If you're dressed shabby like these guys and you go to a regular church, about five guys watch you real close as they pass the plate.'"

▲ The Glory Bound Street ministry serves up meals and sermons in this building on Stockton Blvd. in Oak Park.

◀ As this vacation to Maui demonstrates, family outings, unheard of before, became a vital part of the Lourey's lives. Also, the Lord blessed the Lourey's with two boys to make their home even happier.

▶ Valentine's Day, 1987 shows a different expression on their faces. Love, peace and joy - these were still new to Michael and Linda.

◀ In Escondido in 1989, Michael and the Pastor's wife, Diana, appear behind a stack of pancakes at Victory Outreach Rehabilitation home. The pancake breakfast was given to raise funds to help support this home.

▶ Pastor Tony Ponce and Gary believe that the command to "feed my sheep" which Jesus gave, can be taken literally as well as spiritually. The tatoos on Pastor Tony's forearm are reminders that he grew up in the ganglands of Los Angeles.

Here, Michael is surrounded by men at the rehabilitation home. Left to Right they are Pat (director of the home who came from a life of drugs and drug dealing for which he served a prison term and whose veins still have not returned to normal), George a former gang member, now happily married and teaching Bible study, Michael, Troy (Michael's son who found the Lord only a few months earlier) and Jeff (now a painter and a counselor at the rehabilitation home, formerly known as an alchoholic and vicious fighter). These men spent years of their lives on themselves and their addictions but now even children are drawn to the love and care that Jesus has instilled in their hearts.

The Lord led Michael to a beautiful place in Montana the whole family could enjoy while he wrote this book. He and Linda are now planning to settle on a ranch where they can build a place for people to go for rehabilitation. Their plans include everything from teaching personal hygiene and job training to discipleship training. Many of those who will come to know the revolutionary change Christ makes in the lives of believers need to be taught even the "basics" of social behavior.

WHAT IS YOUR PERSONAL RESPONSE?

The picture of a lamp for our feet and a light for our path is truly appropriate. We are walking in a world of darkness and spiritual warfare which needs illumination.[15] The light we need is the truth. Where shall we go to find it but in the Word? God's laws are indeed right. They point us to the need of a savior,[16] and the commandment is indeed pure. It is manifested in our Lord and Savior, Christ Jesus. When we see the truth which is Jesus, our eyes are forever opened.[17]

Praise God! Remember the song Amazing Grace?

"I once was lost, but now I'm found,
was blind and now I see!"

If we look at the verse from Proverbs in terms of today's roads, we can consider the reproofs of instruction to be the warning signs. Without them we could drive off a washed out bridge or come to a dead end at a high rate of speed ending up a splatter on a brick wall. The Word saves us from us!

When we are "born again," we truly do taste the goodness of the Lord, in all His graciousness.[18] We

deserve destruction and He offers life. We deserve
judgment and He offers mercy. Praise God, *"His
mercy endureth forever!"*[19] Just as an infant desires
the milk of his mother's breast, we need the milk of
the Word of God for our survival. God has put in it
all the spiritual nutrition we need for life![20]
Through the Word, we can also teach each other and
help each other to grow in the Lord.

Don't fall into the common trap that many have
before you. Don't decide that the Bible is just a book,
and that you don't need to take it seriously. We are
told that it is the only offensive weapon we have in
fighting against Satan and all his minions.[21]

**4. If I don't study the Bible, will that harm
my faith?**

Matthew 22:29 -

*But Jesus replied to them, You are wrong be-
cause you know neither the Scriptures nor
God's power.*

Romans 10:16-17 -

*But they have not all heeded the Gospel; for
Isaiah says, Lord, who has believed (had faith
in) what he has heard from us? So faith
comes by hearing [what is told], and what is
heard comes by the preaching [of the message
that came from the lips] of Christ (the Messiah Himself).*

John 12:48 -

*Anyone who rejects Me and persistently
sets Me at naught, refusing to accept My*

teachings, has his judge [however]; for the [very] message that I have spoken will itself judge and convict him at the last day.

Hebrews 2:1 & 3 -

Since all this is true, we ought to pay much closer attention than ever to the truths that we have heard, lest in any way we drift past [them] and slip away. How shall we escape [appropriate retribution] if we neglect and refuse to pay attention to such a great salvation [as is now offered to us, letting it drift past us forever]? For it was declared at first by the Lord [Himself], and it was confirmed to us and proved to be real and genuine by those who personally heard [Him speak].

WHAT IS YOUR PERSONAL RESPONSE?

_____
_____
_____
_____
_____

It should be noted that not studying the scriptures will not only slow the growth of faith, it will inevitably cause faith to die. Churches today are full o people who lost their faith years ago, and are living by rules of men and by incorrect teaching by preachers who are not led by the Holy Spirit.[22] Don't be fooled, God's power is not diminished and will not be subjected by our will.[23] Many people

today, even though they have heard the Gospel and
profess to be Christians, do not follow the commandments of our Lord. The modern churches are full of
those who fit this category. A large part of this
problem is that they don't have a habit of regular
study of the Word.[24] Our deliverance and salvation
(these words in the original language of the Bible are
often the same word) are ongoing processes. Therefore, we need the teaching of the Bible to continue
growing in our faith.

John says that if we hear the Word of God, and
reject Jesus and His teaching, we will be judged for
our disobedience by the very Word which we
reject.[25] How can we make sure that we are not in a
disobedient posture if we are not hiding the Word of
God in our hearts?[26]

We are urged to give special attention to the Word
as we are likely to be forgetful hearers,[27] letting His
teaching slip from the position of prominence which
it deserves. How indeed, shall we escape from the
snares and traps of this world and the destruction offered by Satan to those who will follow him, if we do
not know the Word of God intimately? How shall we
know It intimately, if we do not study It?

Feeding our souls and spirits with the food of the
Bible, will insure that we will not fall victim or be
captured by the Tempter or by his tricks.[28] Studying God's word provides, growth, protection, assurance, comfort, peace, and many more benefits.
Studying worldly wisdom offers confusion, questions, sorrow, disillusionment and finally destruction.[29] Which will you choose? Maybe you will

choose to be lazy, floating through life with no com-
mitments and responsibilities. Go ahead. Your end
will be predictable and very unpleasant.[30]   In the
book of Proverbs, Solomon gives many examples of a
life spent in this manner; just look for statements
addressed to fools.

ADDITIONAL SCRIPTURES

1. John 5:39
2. Isaiah 33:6
3. Hebrews 4:12
4. Acts 9:31
5. James 1:25
6. I John 4:1
7. I John 5:13
8. Ephesians 6:17
9. I Peter 5:8
10. Psalms 119:41 & 45
11. Matthew 6:33
12. Ephesians 6:17
13. I Thessalonians 1:5
14. I Thessalonians 5:16-23
15. II Peter 1:19
16. Galatians 3:24
17. Psalm 19:8
18. Psalm 34:8 and 1 Peter 2:3
19. Psalm 106:1
20. Deuteronomy 8:3
21. Ephesians 6:17

22. II Timothy 3:1-17
23. Isaiah 40:25-28
24. Acts 17 :11
25. John 12:48
26. Psalm 119:11
27. James 1:23-24
28. Isaiah 42:21-23
29. Proverbs 14:12
30. Joshua 24:15, Matthew12:30 & Revelation 21:8

STEP EIGHT

Looking back to our early days as Christians, I remember struggling with the concept of prayer and the "how to" of prayer. The concept was the easiest of the two to overcome. We realized that prayer was the way that we were to communicate with God. Once we got that into our thick skulls, we no longer struggled with why it was necessary.

Naturally, we had the normal questions:

- If God knows everything, what should we pray for?
- If He knew the ending of our lives before they began, why should we pray?
- If He is sovereign, and His Will is unchangeable, what should we pray?
- If He knows the desires of our hearts, how should we pray?

As we began to learn of the Lord in His Word, and in the teaching we were getting, these questions came up and in turn were answered. The key to our being inspired to develop a prayer life was our desire to talk with our Savior. Once we realized that prayer was for more than just the satisfaction of our needs, calling for help in emergencies, and for calming our fears, we really began to enjoy our time spent with the Lord in prayer. We discovered in His Word, that the purpose of prayer is for praising, glorifying, edifying, and thanking God. We also discovered the blessing of praying for the needs of others, which is the response that follows becoming attentive to the Spirit of God. When we started praying for others, we found that we could watch the Hand of God move, and have the results of answered prayers on which to dwell.

Since we were learning to trust our lives to the Lord, we found that we needed to pray for our own situations less and less (Matthew 6:25). This opened up more time for praise and thanksgiving, and more time for intercession for others (praying for others). By doing this we gained more and more confidence in prayer as our eyes were focussed on someone other than ourselves.

One of the people who always comes to mind when I think of answered prayer is a sister in the Lord, Lorie. When we first met her, she was having over fifty grand mal seizures a month; she had cancer of the cervix, mental illness, emphysema; her children were in state-ordered foster care, and she was on thirty-five prescription drugs along with state-ordered psychiatric outpatient care. On top of all that she was a Buddhist. Linda and I had been praying that the Lord would show us some new miracles in the lives of others. We met Lorie at one of our fellowship meetings when a pastor of a local Church referred her to us. I guess that she made his congregation too nervous and they didn't want her there. To make a long story short, we almost lost it when she walked in the door. I remember saying, "Lord, are you sure we can handle this?" Here I was, the one asking to see miracles and when He sent us someone that needed miracles, I doubted His omnipotence. You see it was God that was going to perform the necessary miracles, not "us."

Fortunately, His healing and deliverance don't depend on my ability to believe. During that first meeting Lorie kept interrupting and asking a multitude of questions. Afterwards, she came to Linda and me to ask if our Lord would do miracles for her like He had done for us. Our response was to pray and seek the will of God for her situation. We felt that we, as a group, should pray and fast until we received a direct answer from the Lord. I, in all my wisdom, decided that on the following Saturday we would pray for her deliverance and healing. That night we prayed with her to receive salvation and assured her that we would all be there on Saturday to watch the Lord move in a miraculous way. Naturally, we were all surprised when she called us on Friday to tell us that she had thrown all of her medicine down the toilet.

After we got over our initial panic, we asked her why she had done it. "Well," she said, "as I was praying and studying last night, the Lord told me that I was well and that I didn't need that garbage anymore." Imagine that, we had set the agenda and

God had decided to move in His time instead. So much for our over-inflated ego; the Lord was faithful not only to Lorie, but also to us in that He taught us to depend on Him and not on ourselves. To this day Lorie is physically, emotionally, mentally, and spiritually well, Praise the Lord!! She sings songs which the Lord inspires her to write, in the church she and her family attend. Yes, she also got her children back from the foster care homes!

Prayer has taught us to be continually more dependent on God, less concerned for ourselves, always conscious of the prayer needs of others, and to have a vision trained constantly on the glorification of His Kingdom. Not that we are perfect, but we are learning to desire to be more Christ-like.

After having been through the first part of my life and experiencing all the world had to offer. I didn't under any circumstances want to go back to it. I saw prayer as the best method to insure the guidance of the Holy Spirit in my daily life. The Lord has, through his Spirit, made it absolutely clear to me that without His guidance, destruction (which is constantly lurking in the shadows of our lives) would overtake me and cause me to fall right back into the selfmade pit of despair from which He had rescued me.

Having realized the penalty for being a selfmade man, I knew without a doubt that I couldn't trust my life nor my eternity to a bunch of other selfmade men. My after-care group is now, and always will be communication by prayer with the Triune God and by prayerful support of, my brothers and sisters in the Lord Jesus Christ!

This desire to seek God's will in everything I did, caused some of those around me to wonder if I had lost it or what. I would, and still do, pray before starting the car, for parking places (in the LA basin parking is a major concern), before meals regardless of where I am, before and during work, even about which freeway to take to get somewhere (again, in the LA basin that can be a big factor in how long you are on the freeway). Both Christian and non-Christian people around us thought we were a little right of center, but we were seeking to please God. He said to "Pray without ceasing," so if those around us were disconcerted, well, maybe some of it would sink in and the conviction of the Holy Spirit would overtake them, bringing them to salvation, too.

I should say that only some of our Christian friends were bothered by our constant praying. They soon joined in or didn't go with us anymore. Please, don't misunderstand. We weren't trying to be superior to others or to make them uncomfortable. We were trying to follow the teaching of our Lord and Savior. We were and still are careful not to get into prayer habits which would fall into what Jesus rebuked the Pharisees for in Matthew 23:14. Prayer opens us up to the Holy Spirit. He guides us to be Christ-like in our prayers. Jesus set a pattern of prayer which is in the pages of the Bible (Matthew 6:9-13). We would do well to follow it!

STEP EIGHT
DEVELOP A PRAYER LIFE

We are learning to reach God in prayer; just as reading His Word is how we hear from Him, a life centered on prayer is how we talk to Him, praise Him, worship Him, and make our requests known to Him!

The prayer that we put in the introduction of this book was one of the first written prayers that we ever learned. This type of prayer is not the only or the best type of prayer, but it certainly is a kind of prayer that you might find beneficial. There is absolutely nothing wrong with memorized prayer, or prayers written by someone else. Just don't depend on that one type of prayer for all of your prayer life and all of your prayers. If you read a prayer you like, personalize it and use it whenever it seems appropriate. We did and it has helped us to grow.

When you first begin to pray, you might have a problem sustaining a time of prayer more than a few minutes. Don't worry about it; when you first started to walk many years ago, you couldn't sustain that very long, either. The important thing is that you begin and keep at it. If you wait until you are good at praying to start your prayer life, you will never start. You may, at times, experience what can only be the presence of the Lord in your prayer time. Then again, most of the time you may not have any physical evidence that God heard you at the time you prayed. Some prayers are answered years after they are prayed and some are answered with silence. Be assured, though, that every time you pray, God hears and answers; some of His answers may not be what you want or what you expect, but He is always faithful to His Word. We must understand that He loves us as a perfect parent and, therefore, will not give us something we pray for, if it would be harmful to us or will not fit into His will for our lives.

Another problem experienced in prayer is that we are prone to pray for seemingly good things, with the wrong motives. For example, if we pray for a certain woman or man to notice us just so we can satisfy a lust of our eyes or our flesh, we shouldn't expect the answer to be yes! Another common prayer which seems to fall on deaf ears is a prayer which asks the Lord to do something which we should do, but are too lazy or faithless to do. We cannot expect the Lord to bless us financially if we would use that blessing to be lazy and unfruitful in the service of the Lord. When He answers your prayers with a "No" or with silence, and you are disappointed or don't understand, take those feelings to Him in prayer and ask that He help you to overcome them.

Learning to pray will take effort and determination. The ruler of this world, Satan, doesn't like you talking to the Lord. He will interfere in every way he can. When you are trying to pray there will be interruptions, wrong thoughts, sleepiness, distractions and many other things. If you make a determination to pray a certain amount of time every morning or whenever you feel will be best, do it no matter what.

Don't let Satan steal your joy and your blessings.
Like Bible study, prayer time will become very vital
to your day and will cause you to grow in your ability
to serve the Risen Lord. Will you begin today, or will
you wait and never start? **He is waiting!!!**

As you are learning, don't be concerned about mistakes; as a wise man said, "The way to avoid mistakes is get experience, and the way to get experience is to make mistakes; go forward!" Jesus is always there!

1. Where and when should I pray?

Matthew 6:6 -

*But when you pray, go into your [most]
private room, and, closing the door, pray to
your Father, Who is in secret; and your
Father, Who sees in secret, will reward you in
the open.*

James 5:13 -

*Is anyone among you afflicted (ill-treated,
suffering evil)? He should pray. Is anyone
glad at heart? He should sing praise [to God].*

Acts 12:5 -

*So Peter was kept in prison, but fervent prayer
for him was persistently made to God by the
church (assembly).*

Mark 1:35 -

*And in the morning, long before daylight, He
got up and went out to a deserted place, and
there He prayed.*

Mark 6:46 -

And after He had taken leave of them, He went off into the hills to pray.

Luke 6:12 -

Now in those days it occurred that He went up into a mountain to pray, and spent the whole night in prayer to God.

I Thessalonians 5:17 -

Be unceasing in prayer [praying perseveringly]

WHAT IS YOUR PERSONAL RESPONSE?

_____
_____
_____
_____
_____
_____

The first three types of prayer we listed are different kinds of "where" prayers, not necessarily in a sense of a place, but in the sense of who is involved. Much of your daily prayer life, in fact the vast majority is going to be the first type. The example of a closet is figurative. What you need to do is go somewhere by yourself. Other people will interrupt you and if you have a radio or television on, you will not be able to concentrate. Argue if you will, but I'm right. I've seen too many examples to be convinced otherwise. Most of our daily prayers are private between the Father and us anyway, so

the need for privacy will help you to unburden
yourself.

The second is an example of corporate prayer (a
specific group of people who gather together agreeing together about a specific prayer need). In this
example, we are talking about the case of sickness.
Many other needs can be addressed by this type of
prayer and you will find many times when praying
with a group about a need you have or for another's
needs will be an exciting time of growth.

The last example is of congregational prayer.
This is probably the most exciting type of prayer in
terms of seeing the hand of God move. I have seen
times when literally an entire community has been
influenced to change their minds by congregational
prayer. Churches have been built when the money,
material, permits, qualified workers, etc., have been
unavailable; only devoted congregational prayer was
available to the membership and the church came
together!

The second group is made up of examples of
"when" prayers. Certainly we do not mean that
these are the only times you should pray. You
should develop your prayer life so that you literally
"Pray without ceasing" (I Thessalonians 5:17).
When we talk about "praying without ceasing," we
are not talking about going to a monastery and
never doing anything except praying. We are speaking of a life which is a prayer directed to our Heavenly Father. We are to pray when we get up, when we
go to bed, when we are about our daily lives, all the
time.

You will find that when you have developed your prayer life to an unceasing prayer, the burden of doing right and making the right decisions is no longer a problem; you will have the guidance of the Holy Spirit to direct your path and to order your steps.[1]

No doubt you are wondering why in the world you should pray to God, when he already knows everything. **Because He said to.** Even though we know intellectually that we should do something, it isn't always easy. But then nothing that is worth anything ever is, is it? Believe me, the good gifts of God,[2] are better than anything that this sleazy world has to offer. His gifts don't tarnish or make you sick!

2. Since God knows all things, why pray?

Matthew 26:41 -

All of you must keep awake (give strict attention, be cautious and active) and watch and pray, that you may not come into temptation. The spirit indeed is willing, but the flesh is weak.

Colossians 4:2 -

Be earnest and unwearied and steadfast in your prayer [life], being [both] alert and intent in [your praying] with thanksgiving.

John 16:24 -

Up to this time you have not asked a [single] thing in My Name [as presenting all that I AM]; but now ask and keep on asking and

you will receive, so that your joy (glad-
ness, delight) may be full and complete.

WHAT IS YOUR PERSONAL RESPONSE?

_____
_____
_____
_____
_____
_____

Among the many reasons for our prayer, the need
for guidance against unseen forces and influences is
at the top of the list.[3] Once we are "born again," we
have a new spirit and are spiritually opposed to sin.
However, our old sin nature is still alive and the war
is on. We must learn to reach God in prayer when we
feel the presence of temptation approaching, not
wait until we are in the midst of it.[4]

Someone once said that we should step from in
front of temptation before we ask the Lord to deliver
us. It makes a lot of sense, doesn't it, if I know that
my flesh would have a problem with lust and alcohol, to stay away from bars which have nude dan-
cers? Whenever temptation rears its ugly head, we
are to flee.[5]

We can pray for healing and we can praise Him
when we are healthy, and we can always offer our
thanksgiving for His mercy and His grace.[6] Now
that we are joint heirs with Christ,[7] if we abide in
Him and He in us, we can ask what we will in His
name, and He will complete it.[8]

This isn't to be construed as a blanket credit account; remember that there are conditions to praying in His name.[9] Read what happened to the Israelites who attempted to rebuke demons in Jesus name, without having Him as their Lord and Savior.[10] We firmly believe that if we are walking properly and are truly abiding in Him and He in us, we can ask for anything and it will be done. The thing to remember is that if we are doing those things and He is living His life through us, we will not ask anything unless it is in the Will of His Father, God.

There will also be times when you will be so distressed or so blessed that you will not have the words to pray, at those times the Holy Spirit will make intercession for you with words that cannot be uttered.[11] Praise God, "His mercy endureth forever!"[12] Even when we don't know how to pray, He sends His Holy Spirit to do it for us.[13]

The next crucial question we will try to answer is whether or not prayer is always answered. There are many more instances to study and you would do well to look for them. They will help you in times of trial and need.

3. Are the prayers of a Christian always answered?

Ezekiel 20:3 -

Son of man, speak to the elders of Israel and say to them, Thus says the Lord God: Have you come to inquire of Me? As I live, says the Lord God, I will not be inquired of by you!

II Corinthians 12:7-9 -

And to keep me from being puffed up and too much elated by the exceeding greatness (preeminence) of these revelations, there was given me a thorn (a splinter) in the flesh, a messenger of Satan, to rack and buffet and harass me, to keep me from being excessively exalted. Three times I called upon the Lord and besought [Him] about this and begged that it might depart from me; But He said to me, My grace (My favor and loving-kindness and mercy) is enough for you [sufficient against any danger and enables you to bear the trouble manfully]; for My strength and power are made perfect (fulfilled and completed) and show themselves most effective in [your] weakness. Therefore, I will all the more gladly glory in my weaknesses and infirmities, that the strength and power of Christ (the Messiah) may rest (yes, may pitch a tent over and dwell) upon me!

Isaiah 65:24 -

And it shall be that before they call I will answer; and while they are yet speaking I will hear.

Psalm 91:15 -

He shall call upon Me, and I will answer him; I will be with him in trouble, I will deliver him and honor him.

John 15:7 -

*If you live in Me [abide vitally united to Me]
and My words remain in you and continue to
live in your hearts, ask whatever you will, and
it shall be done for you.*

WHAT IS YOUR PERSONAL RESPONSE?

_____

_____

_____

_____

_____

_____

In the first scriptures, we see prayers which will
not be heard. When man is in a fallen (unsaved)
state, God generally does not hear or answer his
prayers. In this case, the Israelites had gone so far
into disobedience that the Lord was telling them
that He would no longer listen. If we desire our
prayers to be answered, we must be positionally
right; that is we must acquire the righteousness of
Christ Jesus.[14] Without this righteousness we
might as well spit into the wind.

In the second example, Paul is praying for some
malady to be healed and the Lord is telling him that
God's grace will be enough for his situation. There
are many dead-to-the-flesh, "born again" Christians
today with physical infirmities who have prayed for
healing and have not received it. God is sovereign
and His plan for our life is perfect. If a healing is not
manifested, we know that it would not have been for
our best interests or for the further glorification of

God. After all, glorifying God is what we were
created for in the first place.[15]

There are those today who would have you believe
that if you pray for healing and don't receive it, your
faith must not be sufficient. That's not necessarily
true. What they are trying to do is teach you to have
faith in your faith, not in the Creator. If any teaching
you hear draws your focus away from the Godhead, refuse to listen and flee from its presence.[16]

Next, we see the Lord saying that before we call,
He has planned to do what we ask, He will be with
us always,[17] He will be our strength in times of
trouble and He will never disregard us.[18]

In John 15:7, we see the condition to answered
prayer which I talked about earlier. The importance
of this abiding cannot be over-emphasized.[19] In today's climate of easy believism, many people are trying to find a formula for forcing God to do their
will. It won't work. An easy test to see if we are trying to accomplish this heresy is to ask, "Why do I
want this, is it for me or is it for the Lord?" If you are
being honest, you will be able to throw away your
foolish, time-wasting prayers. There is no box which
God fits in. We must learn that prayer is to teach us
to want what we get, not to get what we want! Are
you ready to begin a career of answered prayer, or do
you insist on being a selfish servant of your flesh?

4. How should I pray?

Luke 18:13 -

But the tax collector, [merely] standing at a
distance, would not even lift up his eyes to

heaven, but kept striking his breast, saying, O God, be favorable (be gracious, be merciful) to me, the especially wicked sinner that I am!

Exodus 4:31 -

And the people believed; and when they heard that the Lord had visited the Israelites, and that He had looked [in compassion] upon their affliction, they bowed their heads and worshipped.

Luke 22:41 -

And He withdrew from them about a stone's throw and knelt down and prayed.

Matthew 26:39 -

And going a little farther, He threw Himself upon the ground on His face and prayed saying, My Father, if it is possible, let this cup pass away from Me; nevertheless, not what I will [not what I desire], but as You will and desire.

WHAT IS YOUR PERSONAL RESPONSE?

_____
_____
_____
_____
_____
_____

Did you notice that in each of our examples the attitude of prayer was humble? Even when Jesus prayed he prayed with an attitude of humility, both in spirit and in His physical posture.[20] We are not saying that you must be on your knees or on your face to pray; that would be difficult to do when you are driving. However, humility should be the watchword when we approach God.[21]

Often, we do find it easier to pray when we are lying face down or on our knees as it somehow seems to enhance our concentration on the task at hand. In the example of Luke 18:13, we see a contrast to the religious person who made a great deal of his prayer in Luke 18:11. God is not impressed by the impotent show of our own righteousness; He is concerned with our acquiring Jesus Christ's righteousness. If you are developing an attitude of unceasing prayer, you will find that you can pray in whatever position you find yourself at the time. The form of our prayer is not as critical as the content.

We will find at times that just a few words will suffice. One night when I was driving on an icy road in eastern Washington and came around a corner to see a group of twelve to fifteen deer standing in the road. They were blinded by my headlights and were too terrified to move. There was no way to avoid hitting them except crashing into the cliff on my right or driving into the Columbia river on my left. We were traveling about forty-five miles an hour and only had the time to say, "Jesus, help us!" Miraculously, we passed through the deer without hitting any of them.

Let us exhort you finally, that you should always make your prayers sincere. Don't play games with God! The only game He plays is truth or consequences! God knows the secret places of our hearts and we cannot hide anything from Him.[23] Will you begin today to develop your prayer life, or will you keep getting ready to start until the moment has passed and Satan has devoured you and your testimony?[24]

ADDITIONAL SCRIPTURES

1. Luke 1:79 and John 16:13
2. Matthew 7:11
3. Ephesians 6:12
4. Matthew 26:41
5. I Timothy 6:9-11
6. James 5:13-15
7. Romans 8:17
8. John 14:14
9. John 15:7
10. Acts 19:13-16
11. Romans 8:26
12. I Chronicles 16:31-36
13. Romans 8:26
14. Philippians 3:9
15. I Corinthians 6:20
16. I Timothy 6:3-5
17. Isaiah 65:25
18. Psalm 91:15
19. John 15:7

20. Matthew 26:39 and Luke 22:41
21. I Peter 5:6
22. Luke 18:9-14
23. Matthew 6:6
24. Ecclesiastes 11:4

STEP NINE

I can still remember the first time I led someone in a sinner's prayer. Certainly I wasn't well schooled or particularly polished in my witness, but fortunately my expertise wasn't the issue. It was only a short time after my conversion. The thrill I experienced was like the best high I'd ever had. The big difference was that when I came down, I wasn't sick.

Witnessing is something that, as a general rule, I was reluctant to do for a number of reasons; mostly cowardice (big tough biker, indeed). I was afraid to confront other people with the truth that the Lord Jesus came into the world to die in order to bring salvation to fallen man. It is His Gospel not mine and my fears were totally unfounded. What a joke, Satan convinced me that even if I did witness, people would not listen, or I would do it "wrong."

There was a flaw in his lies which the Lord revealed as soon as I began praying about this lack of courage. The flaw is that it is not me or my words which will bring someone to acknowledge their need for repentance and their need for salvation. Like the saying goes, "I don't make the food, I just set the table, whether or not people choose to eat it is not my responsibility." As soon as I began to trust the consequences of my witnessing to the Lord, my fears evaporated like so much fog on a hot day.

That is a good example of how Satan will try to confuse us by drawing our eyes off the Lord and onto ourselves. Vision that is pointed inward always leads to discouragement and disappointment. Witnessing the Gospel to others is a wonderful opportunity for us to live from joy to joy, rather than from defeat to defeat!

Another amazing thing I noticed was that if my mind was set to look for a chance to witness, I was much more diligent about avoiding the presence of sin. Even an idiot knows that a compromised witness is worse than no witness at all. Imagine telling someone of the wonders of Christ while you are in the midst of things that even a sinner knows are wrong! Yet today, we see that occuring all the time in Christian circles. How much more effective people could be, if they would just give the Lord all of their prejudices and tendencies to be judgmental.

We, in this country, have become so self-centered and self-concerned, that it is amazing if anyone ever notices that people are hurting and need help! I found that if I was looking for some need to fill or some hurt to help, I had little time to think about satisfying the base lust of my flesh. Shortly, the desire to share and witness my conversion and the joy of the Lord, became more important to my life than the struggle of overcoming some of the desires I knew I must overcome. The Lord will help anyone who will call on Him, whether it is to help us overcome our selfish nature, or to teach us how to be effective witnesses to His Glory. He will also help us to overcome our fear of confronting others in their time of need.

When I began to get in tune with the Holy Spirit's urging, I started to notice that the things I said amazed me. When we trust Him to guide and direct our paths as well as our tongues, we will find that He is absolutely trustworthy. More and more, I was amazed by the power of the Holy Spirit to convict people I would have passed by, if I hadn't been listening for His leading. Some of the opportunities for witnessing came at the most unexpected times and places.

For instance, one time I was in a car waiting for my wife to come out of a store. I saw a man sitting in another car and there were tears streaming down his face. After I fought off my cowardice, I went over and asked him if there was anything I could do. The man at first was suspicious, but then decided to talk. He had just lost his job and was newly divorced. Alcohol and drugs were, in his mind, what caused both of those problems and he was contemplating suicide. Praise God, he was desperate enough to listen to the Good News of Christ Jesus. Later that day, I took him to a rescue mission where I was involved in drug and alcohol counseling (as a counselor) and enrolled him in their 90-day program. At last report, he was still doing well and learning to follow Jesus. What if I had not had the habit of looking for opportunities to witness, what would have been the fate of that man? Would his blood have been on my hands as the Prophet Ezekiel warns in Ezekiel 33?

Another time I would have missed the opportunity to witness was at a Salvation Army Men's
Resource Center. It was Christmas Eve and we had
just finished doing an evening of musical praise and
worship for the men there. At the conclusion of the
evening I had delivered a message about having no
room for Jesus. After we led the men in prayer I
noticed a very dishevelled man standing against the
wall in back. Maybe I could have thought that he
heard enough in the message and that if he wanted
help that he could come forward. However, there
was the unmistakable urging of the Holy Spirit to go
to that man and talk to him. I remembered seeing
him come in earlier and wondered how someone
could be in such bad shape and still live. He could
hardly walk, hadn't had a bath in at least several
months, couldn't talk, and was shaking so violently
that he couldn't hold a cup of coffee without spilling
it all over.

When I started talking to him, I discovered that
he hadn't eaten for over a week and that he had been
drunk for the better part of forty years. Some part of
the message had gotten through, as he managed to
make me understand that he wanted to give Jesus
room in his heart and to be forgiven for all of his sins.
Today Gerald (who is about 58) is still sober and is
working tirelessly for the Lord. Now he can talk
(however he will only talk about Jesus), he can walk,
and he works in a street church in Sacramento,
California. Gerald hasn't had a drink since that
night and has never been in a treatment facility. I
guess the Lord is able, after all, to heal and deliver

without all of our worldly devices and without our help.

When you begin to be a witness for the Lord and for His Kingdom, you will find that it offers a truly joyous opportunity to share in the *Wonderworking Power* that He (Jesus) wields. I am reminded of something a sales trainer I knew once said, "Do something, even if it is wrong!" The idea is to get off the starting blocks and begin the race; if you don't, before long the race will be over and it will be too late. Don't wait until you have it down pat or until you graduate from Bible college and have yourself so confused that you don't know where to start. Start right now, right here, right where you are. Chances are your neighbors and friends need the Lord as badly as you did. If you were loved by the Lord enough for Him to save you, aren't they?

STEP NINE
WITNESS YOUR EXPERIENCE TO OTHERS

We know that just as we keep our muscles in shape by exercise, we can keep our spiritual lives in tune by witnessing our experiences to others. We have discovered that one of the greatest thrills in life is helping someone else to find the joy and freedom which we have found in Christ Jesus.

There are a few key points that should be discussed regarding witnessing to unsaved or backslidden people. We need to realize that helter-skelter multiplication of words will accomplish nothing. We need the leading and prompting of the Holy Spirit to be effective and we need to be aware of our ability to relate.

A mode of witnessing which seems to be widely ignored today is the witness of our life. Say what you will with your mouth, if your life doesn't line up, it will make your mouth a liar. Maybe you remember the early seventies. Jesus freaks were on every street corner it seemed, grabbing everyone who walked by. Their message probably was genuine, but not many wanted to hear it. The message their lives seemed to convey was "I used to be all messed up on drugs, but now I'm all messed up on the Lord."

If you feel uncomfortable around professional people, don't go where they are to witness. Conversely, if you don't relate well to street people, don't attempt to be a witness to them. The Lord knows where and when we should be talking; let's let Him be in charge and we will be amazed by the results.

You don't have to be a biblical scholar to be effective in spreading the Gospel, but you should possess some basic knowledge of what you are trying to relate. If you lack experience talking to people you don't know, go with someone else who can, so you can watch and learn, or begin by witnessing to people you already know. Always remember that the consequences are the Lord's responsibility and you will experience far less stress over your witnessing.

Don't, however, go about wildly grabbing people trying to force your message on them. I know that is redundant, but we cannot emphasize enough the importance of the leading of the Spirit. When you find people who are receptive to the message of the Gospel of Christ, pray with them. You don't need to take them to a pastor or some other person in the ministry. Find a simple sinner's prayer that you can memorize and use it. You will miss a tremendous thrill and many blessings by not having the courage to pray others through to the *Family of God.*

After you have prayed the sinner's prayer with a new convert, be sure that they get grounded in their new faith, and that they understand the need to become involved in a local church. Don't sow seeds in the rocks or among the tares. With a little practice and some help from one of your Christian friends, you can become an effective witness for Christ. Don't miss this chance to bless the Kingdom of God, and to bear fruit for the Lord. We will all be held accountable for the character of our life after conversion. Don't be found lacking or with the blood of some sinner on your hands. When the Spirit gives you the chance to witness the Gospel, go for it. You may find that you love it and that you are very proficient at it.

1. How and where should I witness?

Mark 5:19 -

But Jesus refused to permit him, but said to him, Go home to your own [family and relatives and friends] and bring back word to them of how much the Lord has done for you,

and *[how He has]* had sympathy for you and
mercy on you.

Acts 5:20 -

*Go, take your stand in the temple courts and
declare to the people the whole doctrine concerning this Life (the eternal life which Christ
revealed).*

Acts 1:8 -

*But you shall receive power (ability, efficien-
cy, and might) when the Holy Spirit has come
upon you, and you shall be My witnesses in
Jerusalem and all Judea and Samaria and
to the ends (the very bounds) of the earth.*

Psalm 107:2 -

*Let the redeemed of the Lord say so, whom He
has delivered from the hand of the adversary.*

Isaiah 62:6 -

*I have set watchmen upon your walls, O
Jerusalem, who will never hold their peace
day or night; you who [are His servants and
by your prayers] put the Lord in remembrance
[of His promises], keep not silence.*

WHAT IS YOUR PERSONAL RESPONSE?

_____
_____
_____
_____
_____

One of the best examples of when we should witness is given to us in Psalm 107:1, 2, 10-14, 16-18 and 20,

> *O give thanks to the Lord, for He is good; for His mercy and loving kindness endure forever! Let the redeemed of the Lord say so, whom He has delivered from the hand of the adversary.*

> *Some sat in darkness and in the shadow of death, being bound in affliction and in irons [Luke 1:79] because they had rebelled against the words of God and spurned the counsel of the Most High. Therefore He bowed down their hearts with hard labor; they stumbled and fell down, and there was none to help. Then they cried to the Lord in their trouble, and He saved them out of their distresses. He brought them out of darkness and the shadow of death and broke apart the bonds that held them [Psalm 68:6; Acts 12:7, 16:26]!*

> *For He has broken the gates of bronze and cut the bars of iron apart. Some are fools [made ill] because of the way of their transgressions and are afflicted because of their iniquities. They loathe every kind of food, and they draw near to the gates of death.*

> *He sends forth His word and heals them and rescues them from the pit and destruction [Matthew 8:8]*

This is the story of any one of us who was in bondage to our compulsion. The details may change but

the story remains the same. Have we suffered
enough yet, or do we need to be kicked around by the
adversary some more? The same story is told in
Mark 5:19; God is waiting with a compassionate
heart for us to cry out to Him. We are to speak of the
Lord in the churches and to the ends of the earth,
wherever and whenever He chooses to send us! As
we have stated before, we are all watchmen,[1] appointed to proclaim the *Good News of Christ* and to
never keep quiet about the *Glory of God!* Remember
though, if you go out on your own, without the unc-
tion of the Holy Spirit, you will be "as the sound of
cymbals and brass."[2]

2. What is witnessing?

Acts 22:15 -

*For you will be His witness unto all men of
everything that you have seen and heard.*

Philippians 1:27 -

*Only be sure as citizens so to conduct your-
selves [that] your manner of life [will be] worthy of the good news (the Gospel) of Christ, so
that whether I [do] come and see you or am
absent, I may hear this of you: that you are
standing firm in united spirit and purpose,
striving side by side and contending with
a single mind for the faith of the glad tidings
(the Gospel).*

I Corinthians 9:22 -

*To the weak (wanting in discernment) I have
become weak (wanting in discernment) that I*

*might win the weak and overscrupulous. I
have [in short] become all things to all men,
that I might by all means (at all costs and in
any and every way) save some [by winning
them to faith in Jesus Christ].*

II Corinthians 4:5 -

*For what we preach is not ourselves but Jesus
Christ as Lord, and ourselves [merely] as your
servants (slaves) for Jesus' sake.*

WHAT IS YOUR PERSONAL RESPONSE?

_____
_____
_____
_____
_____
_____

We should witness not only our personal experiences, but also the truth of scripture as the Lord
reveals it to us in the Bible. Repeating our own testimony over and over again becomes boring (the part
before we met the *Risen Lord*) very quickly. I have
gotten so tired of hearing of all of my foolishness as a
heathen, that it has become hard to convince myself
to talk about it. The testimony after salvation,
however, is a joy and a blessing that never grows
old.[3] It really becomes special when you can talk
about what the Lord has privileged you to see and
other lives that He is touching.

Many times, we will see the fruit of our labor for
the Lord and will be richly blessed in our spirits by

it. Somehow the miracles in other people's lives seem more exciting than those in our own. In I Corinthians 9:22, Paul is telling us to be sure to talk to people on their level. When you go fishing, do you put something on the hook that you like to eat, or do you use fish bait? When we are fishing for men, we should use the same theory.

Most of all, be sure that you don't fall into the trap of believing that *you* are going to save anyone. It is the *Name of Jesus* which saves, not ours.[4] Many times you will find that being a good listener is more valuable than being a good talker.[5] You can literally listen a person into the *Kingdom of God.* By listening, you can find where they hurt and offer the appropriate *Words of God,* for their situation.

3. Why should I witness?

Mark 16:15 & 16 -

And He said to them, Go into all the world and preach and publish openly the good news (the Gospel) to every creature [of the whole human race]. He who believes [who adheres to and trusts in and relies on the Gospel and Him Whom it sets forth] and is baptized will be saved [from the penalty of eternal death]; but he who does not believe [who does not adhere to and trust in and rely on the Gospel and Him Whom it sets forth] will be condemned.

Matthew 28:19 & 20 -

Go then and make disciples of all the nations, baptizing them into the name of the

Father and of the Son and of the Holy Spirit. Teaching them to observe everything that I have commanded you, and behold, I am with you all the days (perpetually uniformly, and on every occasion), to the [very] close and consummation of the age.

Matthew 24:14 -

And this good news of the kingdom (the Gospel) will be preached throughout the whole world as a testimony to all the nations, and then will come the end.

Ezekiel 33:8 & 9 -

When I say to the wicked, O wicked man, you shall surely die, and you do not speak to warn the wicked from his way, that wicked man shall die in his perversity and iniquity, but his blood will I require at your hand. But if you warn the wicked to turn from his evil way and he does not turn from his evil way, he shall die in his iniquity, but you will have saved your life.

WHAT IS YOUR PERSONAL RESPONSE?

_____
_____
_____
_____
_____
_____
_____
_____

Obviously, we are to witness because God commanded it. However, there are some other compelling reasons for witnessing about our faith. We, as converts to belief in Christ as our Lord and Savior, should be uncomfortable at the thought of anyone going to hell for an eternity and missing the fellowship of our Lord now and forever more.

We can also use our witness as a teaching tool for new converts and for backslidden Christians wherever we go. We are assured that if we are doing His will, we will not be cut off as unproductive branches of the vine.[6]

Many believe that the Lord will not come until the Gospel has been preached to every living person on the earth. We don't agree, but they have the right to be wrong. According to the book of Revelation, the second coming is now at hand. All prophecy has been fulfilled prior to His return. The preaching of the Gospel to every creature will be accomplished during the tribulation, and we won't be here! We will be at the marriage supper of the Lamb![7]

One fact of witnessing or failing to witness is brought up in our last scripture reference in this section. The Lord told the prophet Ezekiel that he was to warn the people that they were responsible for the souls of those who were supposed to hear their witness.[8] If they did witness faithfully, and the wicked didn't turn from their sins, the blood wouldn't be on their hands.[9] If they failed to share their faith and the sinner died in his sins, guess who was responsible? Will you be responsible for the blood of sinners, or will you be faithful to the call of the Lord?[10]

4. When should I share my faith?

Malachi 3:16 -

Then those who feared the Lord talked often one to another; and the Lord listened and heard it, and a book of remembrance was written before Him of those who reverenced and worshipfully feared the Lord and who thought on His name.

I Peter 3:15 -

But in your hearts set Christ apart as holy [and acknowledge Him] as Lord. Always be ready to give a logical defense to anyone who asks you to account for the hope that is in you, but do it courteously and respectfully.

Acts 26:22 -

[But] to this day I have had the help which comes from God [as my ally], and so I stand here testifying to small and great alike, asserting nothing beyond what the prophets and Moses declared would come to pass.

II Timothy 4:2 -

Herald and preach the Word! Keep your sense of urgency [stand by, be at hand and ready], whether the opportunity seems to be favorable or unfavorable. [Whether it is convenient or inconvenient, whether it is welcome or unwelcome, you as preacher of the Word are to show people in what way their lives are wrong].

*And convince them rebuking and correcting,
warning and urging and encouraging them,
being unflagging and inexhaustible in patience and teaching.*

WHAT IS YOUR PERSONAL RESPONSE?

_____

_____

_____

_____

_____

_____

There is a great deal of enjoyment during times
spent with fellow Christians sharing what the Lord
has done and what He is doing in our lives. We can
even be comforted by this fellowship in times of testing and trial.[11] What we think is almost unbearable
usually loses some of its sting when we share it with
our brothers and sisters in the Lord. Normally, we
can find someone who has experienced something
similar and their experience will give us hope.

Another time that sharing our faith can be enjoyable is when someone who is around you a lot asks,
"What is wrong with you. You are always smiling
and filled with joy." Then we can brag about our
Lord and what a wonder He is! That type of witness
plants powerful seeds in the mind of people who, at
best, pretend to have fun once in a while. Always
remember, don't come off like some superior type of
religious saint who has something few can ever hope
to attain.[12] Paul expresses his willingness to do the

work of the Lord as "a reasonable service," not as a burdensome obligation.[13] After all, Jesus rescued us from a life of misery and frustration, and an eternity in the torment of separation from God, the Father.

We are also encouraged to be ready to witness on a moment's notice, whether we expect it or not.[14] We are also told to offer correction to other believers and non-believers always in love, patience and only with scriptural doctrine. Any other advice will ultimately lead to death[15] and destruction. We don't need that type of record on our account when we stand before Him to have our works judged.[16]

Are there any excuses left for not starting today to develop a habit of witnessing our faith? If not, let's get started. If there are, continue in the Word and in prayer until all obstacles are removed and then get busy! Remember, you aren't defeated until you quit.

ADDITIONAL SCRIPTURES

1. Ezekiel 33:2 & 3
2. 1 John 2:18-20
3. Psalm 107:6-8
4. Acts 4:12
5. James 1:19
6. John 15:5 & 6
7. Revelation 19:7
8. Ezekiel 33:6
9. Ezekiel 33:9

10. John 6:44 & Romans 10:13-15
11. Hebrews 10:23-25
12. I Peter 4:3-5
13. Romans 12:1
14. II Timothy 4:2
15. Proverbs 14:12
16. Revelation 20:11-15

STEP TEN

If experiencing temptation is a sin, I would have to spend all my time repenting before the Lord over my wickedness and weaknesses. Fortunately, the deliverance I received was from compulsions. When you are burdened with as many as I was, that is a life-changing experience.

However, the Lord never promised us that we wouldn't be in the presence of sin while we are in this world. When Jesus gave His life as a ransom for our sins on Calvary's Hill, He destroyed two of the three properties of sin for us. The two He destroyed were, the power of sin and the penalty of sin. The presence of sin is a matter we still face today. Sin will always be with us in this world and we must learn to resist it. What the Lord did for me, He will do for you, if you are truly repentant and have accepted His Lordship for your life.

Ever since that first day at the altar, He has given me the ability to resist temptation when it comes. If a particular temptation comes at me, He will make for me "a way of escape," just as He promised. After resisting temptation in a specific area for a sufficient length of time, the temptation starts to fade until it is gone from my life for that particular period of time.

Immediately after my conversion, Satan began working to destroy my "new life." The good news is that Jesus was there to help me to resist temptations which had always overcome me in the past. You see, the problem wasn't that I didn't have any will-power, it was that I didn't have any "won't" power! People used to say, "Yeah, let's get Mikey, he'll do it; Mikey will do anything." A Bible verse which impacted me and helped me in the early going of the battles with temptation is James 1:14-16,

> "But every person is tempted when he is drawn away, enticed and baited by his own evil desire (lust, passions). Then the evil desire, when it has conceived, gives birth to sin, and sin when it is fully matured, brings forth death. Do not be misled, my beloved brethren."

I guess you could say that this verse was the ammunition I needed to resist the whisperings of Satan, when he tried to tempt me to do or say something that I knew in my spirit was wrong. I would stop the process by prayer before it got past the temptation stage. I did find in this passage a circumstance under which I believe that abortion is not only acceptable but good. At the moment when temptation becomes desire and is conceiving the schemes and plots for sin, abort the entire mess by reaching out to God in prayer.

Each time, with the Lord's help and guidance, I was able to overcome a temptation, the next one in that same area was easier and the next even easier still. I should make it clear, that the temptations I did, and still do encounter are not temptations to go back to my old compulsions. The deliverance I received in those areas was permanent and they are no longer a problem. It may shock you to hear someone say that alcoholism and drug addiction can be permanently destroyed, but the Word of God says, "Who the Lord sets free is free indeed." It doesn't have a disclaimer stating that alcoholism, drug addiction, gambling, overeating, and so on are excluded. As the prophet said in the Old Testament, "If God be God, then serve Him!" We, as Christians, must quit putting the Almighty God in a box made by human hands.

Areas in my life that I thought I could never control, I found that Jesus had no problem controlling! As I developed a history of overcoming temptation, I began to believe that each new area would be no more difficult for Jesus to gain a victory over than any of the others. I found that if I rejoiced each time an area of temptation was resisted successfully, I had more courage to face whatever was next. I have found that if we will share our victories with our brothers and sisters in the Lord, not only will we be strengthened, but they will also gain confidence in their battles. We, as Christians, have a tendency to report ONLY bad news. Praise reports are a wonderful gift that the Lord has given us to help to encourage and exhort our brethren.

I can remember several times when I had called someone to tell them of some victory for the Lord, and they later told me that the praise report was exactly the help they needed right then. Linda and I found that using steps six through eight was very helpful in this area of our growth. We came to view them as the tripod of our faith and they have served us well in the battles we have faced.

The Lord doesn't promise that if we accept Him, we will forever be free from the rottenness of this world, He promises us that He will help us to overcome it. Steps six through eight are very good at helping us keep our eye on Him and not on ourselves. I firmly believe that we should glance at our problems and gaze at our Savior, not do what the world would tell us and gaze at our problems and glance at our Savior.

Over the years, we have found Satan to be a relentless adversary, and the Lord to be a perfect leader. At present, the character of our temptations is entirely different than it used to be, but the fact is, temptation is still there. The difference is that we have steadily become more aware of our need to be totally dependent on the Lord to keep us from falling back into our old sins and habits. The more we trust Him the more trustworthy He shows Himself to be! I can truly say that in all the battles we have faced, the Lord has never let us down or turned away. Any turning away that has been done, has been done by us.

There are many stories I could tell you that would demonstrate God's love for each of us, but I'll relate just one. I met a man named Don at a rescue mission. Don had been drinking and doing drugs for a long enough period of time that his entire life was a shambles. His wife had long since left, his children didn't want anything to do with him, he couldn't get or hold a job, and he had no friends left anywhere.

As we talked, Don revealed to me that he had started out years ago as a young married man and a member of a nice little church in Southern California. He started having problems when he and his wife got their first T.V. It seems that the temptation to watch sports on T.V. started to cause him to miss an occasional fellowship or church service. If everything had stopped there, no real problems would have existed. However, they didn't; as is common to most of us, bad habits have a way of starting small and snowballing until they are out of control.

When missing a few meetings didn't appear to hurt anything, he missed a few more and started to bet on different events. Eventually, he ended up hanging around a sports bar and having just a few drinks. One thing led to another and after quite a few years, Don and I were talking about his ruined life. That afternoon, I shared with him how the Lord was waiting with open arms for him to return and that the Lord's forgiveness is always available if we want it. A few days later, Don decided to find out for himself if I was telling the truth.

Today, Don is back with his wife, his children want to be around him again, he has more friends than he can count, and he spends his time working with men and women whose lives have been destroyed like his was. Praise God, He forgives repented sin and you can turn back to Him right now!

STEP TEN
RESIST THE WICKED ONE

We know that experiencing temptation is not a sin. It becomes sin when we respond to it in the wrong way. We found that we can learn how to deal with it in Steps Six, Seven and Eight!

Resisting temptation is a problem which faces all who come to Christ Jesus for salvation and deliverance. It is not simply the domain of the super sinner. My wife, Linda, is a good example of that. Before we were saved, Linda was perfect; at least, we both thought so. If you disagreed, she would argue you into submission. She didn't smoke, drink, use drugs, cuss, or any of the other "major" sins. She soon found out that temptation would be a problem for her as well. It would just be a different type. She would battle with learning to submit and be humble, areas the Lord had already brought me through.

The earliest scriptural mention of resisting temptation is found in Genesis 4:6 & 7,

And the Lord said to Cain, Why are you angry? And why do you look sad and

depressed and dejected? If you do well, will
you not be accepted? And if you do not do
well, sin crouches at your door; its desire is for
you, but you must master it.

Those words are just as appropriate for each of us today as they were for Cain thousands of years ago. In bringing the offering he did, Cain denied that he was a sinful creature under the sentence of divine condemnation. He insisted on approaching God on the ground of personal worthiness. We are still doing exactly that even today! Instead of accepting God's way, he offered God the fruits of the ground which God had cursed. He presented the product of his own toil, the work of his own hands. He wanted to be accepted on the grounds of his own righteousness. Just as He will today, God refused the offering and the results were death and destruction.

The key in these verses is the fact that God tells Cain that sin crouches at his door, but he must learn to resist it. In that respect, absolutely nothing has changed. We are in the same position. The advantage we have is that we have Jesus as our advocate before the Father and since Jesus ascended to the heavenlies, we have the Holy Spirit who never stops trying to guide us.

When temptation becomes such that we think that we are about to break, we have only to turn again to God through fellowship, Bible study and prayer, and we will have an abundance of help in our hour of need. Jesus promised that He would never leave us or forsake us. We must make sure that we are not turning our backs on Him by leaning on our

own understanding. You will find that God's offer of
wisdom (to anyone who asks) will help you with
much of the temptation you will face. All good gifts
come from Him and He will give freely to those who
are in need if they will only ask. A little prayer will
often help us in the moments of our greatest trials;
try asking God to *bless* the activity you are about to
indulge in. This will open you up to the *Power and
Might* of the Holy Spirit and will usually keep you
from making a dire mistake. If God has delivered
you, you are free, don't be a fool and go back to find
out. Your "new life" is like a suit of clothes, put it on
daily, or go back to your vomit!

1. When I resist, what will happen?

James 4:7 -

*So be subject to God. Resist the devil [stand
firm against him], and he will flee from you.*

I Peter 5:8-10 -

*Be well balanced (temperate, sober of mind),
be vigilant and cautious at all times; for that
enemy of yours, the devil, roams around like a
lion roaring [in fierce hunger], seeking someone to seize upon and devour. Withstand
him; be firm in faith [against his onset -
rooted, established, strong, immovable, and
determined], knowing that the same (identi-
cal) sufferings are appointed to your brother-
hood (the whole body of Christians) throughout the world. And after you have suffered a
little while, the God of all grace [Who imparts
all blessing and favor], Who has called you to*

His [own] eternal glory in Christ Jesus, will Himself complete and make you what you ought to be, establish and ground you securely, and strengthen, and settle you.

James 1:12 -

Blessed (happy, to be envied) is the man who is patient under trial and stands up under temptation, for when he has stood the test and been approved, he will receive [the victor's] crown of life which God has promised to those who love Him.

Revelation 3:21 -

He who overcomes (is victorious), I will grant him to sit beside Me on My throne, as I Myself overcame (was victorious) and sat down beside My Father on His throne.

WHAT IS YOUR PERSONAL RESPONSE?

_____

_____

_____

_____

_____

What a promise, if we resist (and keep on resisting) Satan will be forced to flee. The concept of ongoing resistance is important because if we get the idea that we only have to resist the first time we are tempted, it won't be long until we are right back in the mess that the Lord rescued us from.

- We also have certain promises if we will be steadfast in our resistance.[1]

- Even though Satan is relentless and vicious,[2] we are not the first nor the last to depend on Jesus to help us to resist.

- How wonderful to know that Jesus has been defeating him all of the time and will continue to do so for us today.[3]

- God also will, after we overcome temptation, finish our faith, ground us firmly in His will, and make us strong and well established.[4]

- The concept that temptation must be endured is very accurate. It is not easy, but with perseverance we will be successful.[5]

- Our crown of eternal life is waiting for us at the other end of our journey. Is it worth it? *YOU CAN COUNT ON IT!*

- The last promise is abundantly wonderful when you understand it! We will actually be able to sit on the *Throne of Christ* and God will not cause us to be moved.[6]

- Imagine that! Or would you prefer to sit on the throne prepared for Satan in the *Lake of Fire*?[7]

   Which will you choose?

2. Can Satan force me to sin?

I Corinthians 10:13 -

For no temptation (no trial regarded as enticing to sin, no matter how it comes or where it leads) has overtaken you and laid hold on you that is not common to man [that is, no temptation or trial has come to you that is beyond human resistance and that is not adjusted and adapted and belonging to human experience, and such as man can bear]. But God is faithful [to His Word and to His compassionate nature], and He [can be trusted] not to let you be tempted and tried and assayed beyond your ability and strength of resistance and power to endure, but with the temptation He will [always] also provide the way out (the means of escape to a landing place), that you may be capable and strong and powerful to bear up under it patiently.

Ephesians 6:12 & 13 -

For we are not wrestling with flesh and blood [contending only with physical opponents], but against the despotisms, against the powers, against [the master spirits who are] the world rulers of this present darkness, against the spirit forces of wickedness in the heavenly (supernatural) sphere. Therefore put on God's complete armor, that you may be able to resist and stand your ground on the evil day [of danger], and, having done all [the crisis demands], to stand [firmly in your place].

II Corinthians 10:4 & 5 -

For the weapons of our warfare are not physical [weapons of flesh and blood], but they are mighty before God for the overthrow and

destruction of strongholds. [Inasmuch as we]
refute arguments and theories and reasonings
and every proud and lofty thing that sets itself
up against the [true] knowledge of God; and
we lead every thought and purpose away cap-
tive into the obedience of Christ (the Messiah,
the Anointed One).

I John 5:18 -

We know [absolutely] that anyone born of God
does not [deliberately and knowingly] practice
committing sin, but the One Who was begot-
ten of God carefully watches over and protects
him [Christ's divine presence within him
preserves him against the evil], and the wick-
ed one does not lay hold (get a grip) on
him or touch [him].

WHAT IS YOUR PERSONAL RESPONSE?

_____
_____
_____
_____
_____
_____

God uses times of temptation to cause us to grow
and to cause us to learn that we are His creations.
When Adam sold our birthright in the Garden of
Eden,[8] we were still His creation, we just needed a
redeemer. In His love, He sent His Son Jesus to die
for our sins[9] thereby redeeming our lost position
with Him. We are never tempted beyond what He

already knows that we can endure. Remember, He is omniscient; He knows the end of our days before the beginning. He will also cause us to grow as we learn to see our escape from temptation. He has promised to give us an escape if the temptation is beyond our ability to endure.[10]

One of the things we lost when Adam sinned was our ability to see in the spiritual realm. Many today, (even in the church), don't believe that there is a spiritual war going on all around us. However, since God says in His Word that it is there, we know that it is.[11] Probably in our weakness, we are better off not being able to see it; we would most likely lose it and run away, if we could. The tempter will try to cause us to become disobedient to Christ and we must use the weapons which God has provided (prayer, the Word of God, Christian unity) to wage our war. If we try to fight our battles on our own... well, you can see the results by the condition you were in before you met the Lord.

To the many who insist that Satan is a myth and doesn't exist, I say, "Resist him and see what happens, if you have the guts. I should caution you to be sure of your relationship to the Lord Jesus before you do, as the analogy of his being like a raging lion is the truth."[12]

There are those who try to say that I John 5:18 means that if a Christian ever commits one sin, he is not truly "born again." This is another lie propagated by people who speak without knowing the facts; Solomon calls them fools in the book of Proverbs.[13] The original language translated literally says that

if we are born of God, we do not manifest lifestyle sin
and we repent of the individual sins we do commit.
Because of our positional righteousness, Satan cannot force anything on us, but he will tempt, trick,
persuade, and try to coerce us into his traps and
snares. We have the weapons and the knowledge to
cast him off if we will use them or we can continue to
use our own righteousness like Cain did.[14] Take
your pick. You will choose one or the other!

3. Will Jesus always be there to help me?

Matthew 28:20 -

> *Teaching them to observe everything that I
> have commanded you, and behold, I am with
> you all the days (perpetually, uniformly, and
> on every occasion), to the [very] close and con-
> summation of the age. Amen (so let it be).*

Hebrews 13:5 -

> *Let your character or moral disposition be free
> from love of money [including greed, avarice,
> lust, and craving for earthly possessions] and
> be satisfied with your present [circumstances
> and with what you have]; for He [God] Him-
> self has said, I will not in any way fail you nor
> give you up nor leave you without support. [I
> will] not, [I will] not, [I will] not in any degree
> leave you helpless nor forsake nor let [you]
> down (relax My hold on you)! [Assuredly not!]*

II Peter 2:9 -

> *Now if [all these things are true, then be sure]
> the Lord knows how to rescue the godly out of*

*temptations and trials, and how to keep the
ungodly under chastisement until the day of
judgment and doom.*

Colossians 3:3 & 4 -

*For [as far as this world is concerned] you
have died, and your [new, real] life is hidden
with Christ in God. When Christ, Who is our
life, appears, then you also will appear with
Him in [the splendor of His] glory.*

WHAT IS YOUR PERSONAL RESPONSE?

_____
_____
_____
_____
_____
_____

The Lord has promised us that he will always be
with us, but at times we can wonder, especially when
He appears to be silent. At those times when His
silence is deafening, we must take comfort in the
scriptures and in His promises. We know that He
said that He would be faithful, even when we are
not.[15] Don't despair when moments like this seem
to make you feel faithless. The light at the end of the
tunnel is not the headlight of an on-coming train.
When you emerge at the other end of times like that,
you will be stronger and more capable to perform
whatever work He has for you.

Looking back is our evidence of His presence in
those times when we feel alone. Usually when we

are feeling like we are alone, we have been burdened with some guilt trip by the enemy. When that happens, turn to prayer and praise. Satan is allergic to praise and must depart.[16] Often hymns and Christian songs will serve to free you to recognize His love afresh.[17]

Learning to be content will also help you in your battle against the Evil One.[18] If we are constantly thinking of our own petty needs and problems, we fail to perceive the overall picture of the *Kingdom of God*. Be assured, He will supply all of your need![19] He never fails or lies, only we do that! We can know with certainty that His promise to deliver the just and to judge the unjust is real, since we serve a just God.[20]

By reading the history of man in the Bible, we will find many examples of the just being delivered against all possibility. Since He never changed,[21] the promises are still good today! The only way that you will fall victim to evil desires and lusts is if you choose to; not by one all-encompassing gesture, but by a series of small decisions which you knew were wrong when you made them. If you catch yourself asking, "I wonder just how far I can go with this and still not sin," flee from whatever you are doing. Instead ask, "What will this do to build up or edify the Kingdom of God?"[22] The former will lead you to more pain and destruction and the latter will surely lead you into the loving arms of our Father in Heaven. Will you follow man's history, or follow "the Bright Morning Star?"[23]

Revelation 22:12 -

Behold, I am coming soon, and I shall bring my wages and rewards with me, to repay and render to each one just what his own actions and his own work merit.

4. How can I know when Satan is trying to deceive me?

I Corinthians 14:33 -

For He [Who is the source of their prophesying] is not a God of confusion and disorder but of peace and order. As [is the practice] in all the churches of the saints (God's people).

II Timothy 1:7 -

For God did not give us a spirit of timidity (of cowardice, of craven and cringing and fawning fear), but [He has given us a spirit] of power and of love and of calm and well-balanced mind and discipline and self-control.

I John 4:1 -

Beloved, do not put faith in every spirit, but prove (test) the spirits to discover whether they proceed from God; for many false prophets have gone forth into the world.

Galatians 5:19 & 21 -

Now the doings (practices) of the flesh are clear (obvious): they are immorality, impurity, indecency, idolatry, sorcery, enmity, strife, jealousy, anger (ill temper), selfishness, divisions (dissensions), party spirit (factions,

sects with peculiar opinions, heresies), envy,
drunkenness, carousing, and the like. I warn
you beforehand, just as I did previously, that
those who do such things shall not inherit the
kingdom of God.

WHAT IS YOUR PERSONAL RESPONSE?

_____

_____

_____

_____

_____

_____

You can always be certain that if you are confused
about anything, it is not the Spirit of God who is
dealing with you.[24] His dealings are sure and confident. Be careful, though, of adopting the attitude of,
"Well, I have a peace about that, so it must be all
right." Many times, we find that having peace is
another way of saying that we are too lazy or
cowardly to do what we know we are supposed to do.
Don't use peace to wait for the Lord to do something
that He has empowered you to do!

If we are fearful, we need to go to the Lord in
prayer and overcome that trap of Satan.[25] If we are
walking with the Lord, we need not fear anything. If
anything we are doing or are contemplating doing is
characterized by any of these attributes, Satan is
trying to deceive you into sin and destruction. You
can rationalize all you want, but the bottom line is,
SIN IS SIN! Flee from unrighteousness.[26]

ADDITIONAL SCRIPTURES

1. I Corinthians 15:57 & 58
2. Revelation 2:10
3. Colossians 2:14 & 15
4. II Thessalonians 3:3
5. Revelation 3:11
6. Revelation 3:21
7. Matthew 25:41
8. Genesis 3:17-19
9. John 3:16
10. I Corinthians 10:13
11. Ephesians 6:12
12. I Peter 5:8
13. Proverbs 10:21
14. Genesis 4:5
15. II Timothy 2:13
16. James 4:7
17. Psalm 40:3
18. Philippians 4:11-13
19. Philippians 4:19
20. Ecclesiastes 3:17
21. Hebrews 1:12 & James 1:17
22. Romans 6:13
23. I Peter 1:19
24. I Corinthians 14:33
25. I John 4:18
26. I Timothy 6:11 & 12

STEP ELEVEN

After years of never doing anything without the motive of getting a return, learning to be a giver would have been nearly impossible if the Spirit of the Lord had not been residing in me and guiding me. Even at that, giving without selfish interests was hard to comprehend. Linda and I would propose to give something to a certain need and before we could accomplish it, doubt and confusion would creep in. As we have already discussed, doubt and confusion are not attributes of the Holy Spirit, so we knew that the source was Satan, not God. Still the battle was there, but in time we learned to overcome it.

Giving is never easy when you have always been a "taker," but the joy caused by the act of freely giving is worth ten times the struggle. Whenever someone talks about giving, we always tend to think in terms of money. However, Jesus didn't teach that money was what He was interested in. What He did teach was that He wanted our best, and it will always involve more than money. He wants the best of our lives, our time, our love, as well as our money.

In the modern church we have been convinced that God only really desires our money, when if the truth were known, He would tell us that money is the least of His concerns. Why would He, who owns the entire universe and everything in it, need our money? After all, if He is the source of all blessings in the first place, all we are doing is giving back a portion of what He gave us.

In today's society, finding needs wasn't hard; deciding which need to give to was the problem. Doing this took a total dependence on the guidance of the Lord, and trust in Him to know what was best. Naturally, we immediately began to tithe to our home church, right? Sorry to disappoint you, but that was the hardest battle we had to face. Satan kept us fouled up on that matter for a good long while.

At first, tithing appeared to be a matter which comes under the *Law,* and not under *Grace.* Most New Testament references to tithing are rebukes, so we asked questions and rationalized the matter until we were totally confused. We believed that since we were dead to our old lives and alive to Christ, we had given all to Him and would do anything He wanted with our resources. Sounds good, but it didn't work. The Lord kept the issue of tithing in front of us continually until we decided that if Satan was working so hard to stop us from tithing, it was something that we would do without any further discussion.

Funny thing, once we formed that habit, all confusion and doubt left and all of our arguments seemed not to matter anymore. Even if the fact that Satan didn't want us to tithe was our only justification for doing it, that was enough for us. We found that giving ten percent of our income was a good place to start and we have been able to far surpass that as time went by. Now, we give automatically based on our gross income regardless of whatever else seems important. If it appears that we won't have enough left for our needs after tithing, we give anyway and the Lord is always there to make sure our needs are supplied.

Giving love offerings to ministries and people we knew were in need was easy, and is still one of our major sources of joy. We have found at times that the Spirit of God will urge us to give what amounts to everything we have at a given moment. The first few times you do that, you will find that it will make you a little nervous. However, if you will listen and respond to His urging, you will find that there was nothing to be concerned about; in fact, it will be a source of rejoicing when you see the miracles ahead.

Giving without anyone knowing the source of the gift is such a blessing that I cannot even begin to describe it. Since we are confident that all of our needs will be covered, giving is very easy. The look on the face of someone who was in need, without hope and resources is worth more than money or possessions. Despair is changed to joy in receiving an anonymous gift, which is an act of mercy.

The counsel which helped us the most in relation to giving is found in the Bible (where else?) in the book of Ecclesiastes, chapter 11. When you have a moment, study it and then try what Solomon advises and see if he isn't right! As I stated earlier, money is not the most important thing we have to give. Our time, spent in fellowship with our brothers and sisters or ministering to those in need around us, is a crucial part of giving. Whenever I think about giving my time to further the work of the Lord, I think of the many blessings that have resulted from obedience to the urging of the Holy Spirit.

Our love is also important. If Jesus loved us enough to give His life so that we might be saved, how should we respond? When we see a need or a hurt, shouldn't we respond in a Christ-like manner? If we are true disciples of His, we should always strive to respond to every situation as we know He would. Jesus never turned away from those in need because they weren't pretty, clean, pleasant, well-dressed, or even in His social class. Jesus even ministered to the Samaritans who were considered lower than dogs by the Jews of that day. I will admit that learning to be sensitive to other people's needs can be difficult and uncomfortable, but if you will, I promise that you will be more than pleased with His response.

Since we were converted we have moved quite a few times and have always given away our furniture (and anything else we felt we could replace) to people who were in need of it. Some of our friends thought we were nuts, but we did it anyway, just for the joy of it. Naturally, the fact that we were always supplied with replacements when we got where we were going helped us to be willing to give.

I remember one time when Linda felt that the Lord wanted her to give all of her business suits and dresses to a friend who had just been restored by the Lord and was about to go back to work. In all of my spiritual maturity, I wondered how we were going to replace them as we had no extra money at the time. We sat down and figured that it would take about $2,000 to replace what she gave away, and now she had nothing nice to wear. A few days later, another woman whom the Lord had delivered from her bondage to alcohol came over and asked Linda if she would be offended by used clothes. What she had was a bunch of designer suits, dresses, blouses and slacks. They were all clothes she had purchased when she worked in a clothing store and had not worn. What was truly amazing about the gift is that the woman who was giving Linda the clothes was at least three inches taller and about thirty pounds heavier. There is no way clothes that woman bought for herself would fit Linda, right? That wasn't the plan of the Lord; they all fit perfectly. We don't have an explanation for it, we just accept His graciousness whenever and however it comes. Praise God, "His loving kindness endures forever."

No matter how poor we felt in a given situation, we were always able to find someone who was worse off than we were and found a way to give to their need. Giving is now one of my favorite activities; who would have believed it; I wouldn't have!

STEP ELEVEN
BEGIN GIVING

We have determined to give what we should and to discover where and when to give. We have been takers long enough, we will now become givers.

Jesus said, "Freely you have received, freely give." He wasn't talking specifically about money or material substance but the reference applies just the same. Our giving will, in many ways, determine the character of our Christian life. Will we be generous or will we be miserly? Miserly people are miserable. Do you see the similarity in the words? All of us have known at least one miserly person. It's really tragic when that person is a professing Christian. The reason we say "professing Christian" is that miserly characteristics contradict the entire teaching of our Lord.

When you are prompted to give by the Spirit of God, give to the utmost; you will never be disappointed. In the society we live in, this principle is at odds with secular teaching. A motto that seems to fit the modern trend is, "Get all you can; Can all you get, Sit on the can!" That is a tragic way to live as selfishness will be your destruction.

In the eleventh chapter of Ecclesiastes, Solomon advises us to *"Give generously, for your gifts will return to you later. Divide your gifts among many, for in the days ahead you yourself may need much help"* (The Living Bible). Instead of protecting what you have, give! The Amplified Bible reads, *"Cast your bread upon the waters, for you will find it after many days. Give a portion to seven, yes even [divide it] to eight, for you know not what evil may come upon the earth".* This command also holds a precious promise from God, *"...you will find it after many days."*

A very successful man of our times once said that success isn't getting, it is giving. Will you be successful? Learn to give generously. In Proverbs 19:17, Solomon wrote,

> *"He who is gracious to a poor man lends to the Lord, and He will repay him for his good deed"* (KJV)

and conversely in Proverbs 21:13,

> *"He who shuts his ear to the cry of the poor will also cry himself and not be answered"* (KJV)

There is a Christian hymn that is particularly appropriate here,

> *"Face to face with Christ our Saviour,*
> *Face to face what will it be?"*

Only you can answer that. If you don't have money or material possessions, you have time and other resources for which the *Family of God* can find a use! The excuse of, "I don't have anything to give," is a crock. We all have God-given gifts which we can use to benefit others. If we pray to the Lord for the desire in our hearts to become givers, He will cause it to be so! You may find yourself in the midst of misfortune right now; if you look back with an honest appraisal, you will admit that you have shut your ear to a cry from someone in need, haven't you? Maybe you aren't in need yet, but if you take the same inventory you may find the same instances in your past. In either case, repent and begin giving. It is never too late, while you are still alive.

In the scripture we are told that God loves a cheerful giver; the wording in the Greek actually means one who gives hilariously. In other words, give till it makes you laugh with joy, not until it hurts. If you are giving until it hurts, you have the wrong attitude. Take your life to the Lord in prayer, ask Him to show you where to change and what to change, so you can be a cheerful giver!

1. Why should I give?

Acts 20:35 -

In everything I have pointed out to you [by example] that, by working diligently in this manner, we ought to assist the weak, being mindful of the words of the Lord Jesus, how He Himself said, It is more blessed (makes one happier and more to be envied) to give than to receive.

II Corinthians 9:6 & 7 -

[Remember] this: he who sows sparingly and grudgingly will also reap sparingly and grudgingly, and he who sows generously [that

blessings may come to someone] will also reap generously and with blessings. Let each one [give] as he has made up his own mind and purposed in his heart, not reluctantly or sorrowfully or under compulsion, for God loves (He takes pleasure in, prizes above other things, and is unwilling to abandon or to do without) a cheerful (joyous, "prompt to do it") giver [whose heart is in his giving].

Matthew 6:4 -

So that your deeds of charity may be in secret; and your Father Who sees in secret will reward you openly.

Malachi 3:10 -

Bring all the tithes (the whole tenth of your income) into the storehouse, that there may be food in My house, and prove Me now by it, says the Lord of hosts, if I will not open the windows of heaven for you and pour you out a blessing, that there shall not be room enough to receive it.

WHAT IS YOUR PERSONAL RESPONSE?

_____

_____

_____

_____

_____

_____

One of the key issues of the Gospel of Christ is the compassion He had for the poor and the oppressed.[1] We are told repeatedly that we are to bear one another's burdens,[2] give of our substance to support the widows and orphans[3] and never turn the needy away.[4] In our own lives, we invariably find that we get much more joy out of filling another's needs than we do from receiving. Here, we also see that there is a proportionality to our giving. In other words, when we have enough to give, and we do so grudgingly or sparingly, we will receive the same treatment when we are in need.[5]

Many people we have talked to feel that they will never be in need. Don't bet on it. You don't know when or what type of calamity will befall you.[6] You will find that when you can give an anonymous gift, the joy of the gift will more than satisfy you.[7] Don't, however, give an anonymous gift and later decide to divulge the source. You will destroy all of the blessings of the gift by that act of self-centeredness.

The verse in Malachi is one of the most misused scriptures today. Don't give with the idea that if you give, God is obligated to prosper you financially. The "prosperity gospel" which is sweeping the United States today is nothing short of attempted witchcraft and should be avoided. The most valuable blessing you will ever receive will be of a spiritual nature and is the kind the Lord is speaking of in this passage. When you encounter the health and prosperity gospels, flee from the presence of them so that you will not be tempted by Satan to worship some other god.[8]

2. What is tithing?

Leviticus 27:30 -

And all the tithe of the land, whether of the seed of the land or of the fruit of the tree, is the Lord's; it is holy to the Lord.

Numbers 18:21 -

And, behold, I have given the Levites all the tithes in Israel for an inheritance in return for their service which they serve, the [menial] service of the Tent of Meeting.

Deuteronomy 14:22-25 -

You shall surely tithe all the yield of your seed produced by your field each year. And you shall eat before the Lord your God in the place in which He will cause His Name [and Presence] to dwell the tithe (tenth) of your grain, your new wine, your oil, and the firstlings of your herd and your flock, that you may learn [reverently] to fear the Lord your God always. And if the distance is too long for you to carry your tithe, or the place where the Lord your God chooses to set His Name [and Presence] is too far away for you, when the Lord your God has blessed you, then you shall turn it into money, and bind up the money in your hand, and shall go to the place [of worship] which the Lord your God has chosen.

Matthew 23:23 -

Woe to you, scribes and Pharisees, pretenders (hypocrites)! For you give a tenth of your mint and dill and cummin, and have neglected and omitted the weightier (more important) matters of the Law - right and justice and mercy and fidelity. These you ought [particularly] to have done, without neglecting the others.

WHAT IS YOUR PERSONAL RESPONSE?

_____
_____
_____
_____
_____
_____

Within the Christian Church today, tithing is taught as a practice which we are commanded by God to follow. There are, however, a couple of problems with this teaching. First of all, tithing was an ordinance of the Law of God as given to Moses. The Law of Moses was for the children of Israel and not for anyone else. Secondly, the amount of the tithe is a matter of some debate, some saying 10% and others as much as 23-1/3% These arguments are very lengthy and time consuming, therefore, since they are not vital to our Christian walk, they will not be covered here. However, if you would be interested in an in-depth study of these matters there are good materials available.

We are not interested in throwing stones or condemning anyone. We do, however, take issue with what must be seen as heresy. If you are taught that by giving a tithe of your income, or increase, you will obligate God to give you an increased return, do not listen.[10] As we have said, God doesn't fit into any manmade box. His actions are not dependent upon, or subject to, the will of man or man's actions.[11] If we could, by some mumbo-jumbo, force God to do our will, the god we would be worshipping would be weaker than the people who worship him! If that were the case, why would we want him?

New Testament giving is characterized by cheerfulness and[12] generosity,[13] not by law and greed. Study, if you will, Acts 4:32-37 and 5:1-11. Since we are to pattern ourselves after the apostles and the early church, doesn't it follow that we should be willing to do as they did? They did what they did because there was great poverty and need in the churches. They felt it was necessary to obey the urging of the Spirit of God. Do you see a need today? If you do, don't waste any time thinking of what someone else ought to be doing.[14] Decide what you are being urged to do by the Holy Spirit and get after it!

We are not attempting to influence anyone to sell everything they have, or anything else. We are simply saying that as Christians, we should and must be willing to do whatever the Lord requires and to seek the mind of God in everything.[15] Remember, test all spirits.[16] If we are doing what is right in our own eyes,[17] we can be sure that we will not be doing right in the eyes of God. Not only that, but we do have a king, the Lord of Lords and King of Kings, Jesus.[18]

Certainly, we do not advocate that anyone stop giving to their local church and to worthy Christian ministries. The worker is certainly worthy of his hire and we need to support him.[19] Without those who have given over their lives to do the work of the church and it's ministries, we would be in dire straights. They not only deserve our financial support, they need our prayers and our commitment. We encourage you to find a Bible-believing church (that is a church where the Word of God is taught) and become involved in the work of the Gospel. When you do, you can help others who may be in worse condition than you!

3. Should I give more than a tithe?

Matthew 5:42 -

Give to him who keeps on begging from you, and do not turn away from him who would borrow [at interest] from you.

II Corinthians 8:11-12 -

So now finish doing it, that your [enthusiastic] readiness in desiring it may be equalled by your completion of it according to your ability and means. For if the [eager] readiness to give is there, then it is acceptable and welcomed in proportion to what a person has, not according to what he does not have.

Mark 12:44 -

For they all threw in out of their abundance; but she, out of her deep poverty, has put in everything that she had [even] all she had on which to live.

Luke 6:38 -

*Give, and [gifts] will be given to you; good
measure, pressed down, shaken together, and
running over, will they pour into [the pouch
formed by] the bosom [of your robe and used
as a bag]. For with the measure you deal out
[with the measure you use when you con-
fer benefits on others], it will be measured
back to you.*

WHAT IS YOUR PERSONAL RESPONSE?

_____
_____
_____
_____
_____
_____

A willing mind is the key to Christian giving.[20]
Some of the largest givers we have encountered are
giving it out of greed, trying to use God's promises
for personal gain, or out of a sense of obligation.
Both of those types of givers already have their
reward. Learning to be generous (and you will have
to learn) is a worthy task. The Bible teaches us that
sometimes when we are hospitable to strangers in
need, we are actually entertaining angels.[21] When
you have learned to give to those who ask of you, the
assurance of the Lord that your needs will be met,
becomes a reality.[22]

The example from Mark 12:44 (also see Luke 21:2
& 3) is a woman who, giving all she had, trusted the

Lord to keep her. This kind of giving is indeed scriptural, but should be practiced only with the leading
of the Holy Spirit. Remember that Satan can come
disguised as an angel of light,[23] and we are to test
every spirit.[24]   "Give and it shall be given unto
you;"[25] sound advice, however the scripture doesn't
say that if you give money, you will get money. We
have found that when the Lord gives us the gift of a
blessing in our spirit or a time of rejoicing and
praise, we value it much more than a financial blessing.

Money is only a tool and should be treated as
such. It will not solve any problems, contrary to the
world's teaching. It will only give us different
problems to deal with. The joy of the Lord is eternal
and of far superior value. Have you seen the
bumper sticker which reads, "The one who wins
is the one with the most toys"? What the sticker doesn't tell us is that the prize is the booby
prize in a fool's paradise. Don't let material possessions become a god to you; give generously
and find joyous freedom from the cares of this
world!

**4. Along with money is there more I can
give?**

Isaiah 58:6 & 7 -

*[Rather] is not this the fast that I have chosen;
to loose the bonds of wickedness, to undo the
bands of the yoke, to let the oppressed go free,
and that you break every [enslaving] yoke? Is
it not to divide your bread with the hungry*

*and bring the homeless poor into your house -
when you see the naked, that you cover him,
and that you hide not yourself from [the needs
of] your own flesh and blood?*

Matthew 25:34-36 -

*Then the King will say to those at His right
hand, Come, you blessed of My Father [you
favored of God and appointed to eternal sal-
vation], inherit (receive as your own) the
kingdom prepared for you from the founda-
tion of the world. For I was hungry and you
gave Me food, I was thirsty and you gave Me
something to drink, I was a stranger and you
brought Me together with yourselves and
welcomed and entertained and lodged Me.
I was naked and you clothed me, I was
sick and you visited Me with help and
ministering care, I was in prison and you
came to see Me.*

Luke 3:11 -

*And He replied to them, He who has two
tunics (undergarments), let him share with
him who has none; and he who has food, let
him do it the same way.*

James 2:15 & 16 -

*If a brother or sister is poorly clad and lacks
food for each day, and one of you says to him,
Goodbye! Keep [yourself] warm and well fed,
without giving him the necessities for the
body, what good does that do?*

WHAT IS YOUR PERSONAL RESPONSE?

———————————————————————————————
———————————————————————————————
———————————————————————————————
———————————————————————————————
———————————————————————————————
———————————————————————————————

There is something more valuable to the Lord than money. If you are willing to give it, you will indeed be blessed. The thing of value we speak of is your life. Doesn't it seem reasonable that since He gave us a "new life" which contains eternity with Him, we should be willing to give it back to Him? What we mean is that we should surrender our lives and everything to do with them to *His Lordship* to do with as He pleases.[26]

The things we will be doing which please Him, if we make Him Lord of our lives, are stated in Isaiah 58:6 & 7. The scriptures from Matthew 25 and from Luke 3 are reiterations of the same principles. He doesn't want a show of piety, He wants a life devoted to His service, and His concerns. If you are interested in knowing what happens to those of us who decide to become "pew pilots" and selfishly keep a tight grip on our lives, read Matthew 25:41 & 46! Does that make your decision any easier?

Be alert that you don't carelessly fall into the habit of ignoring the needs of others, both in the *Family of God* and among the lost. James is speaking of exactly this in chapter 2:15 & 16; our words of encouragement and our outward show of piety do not profit the *Kingdom of God*. What will profit His Kingdom is our genuine and sincere concern for others. This concern is demonstrated by our willingness and steadfastness to look for a need to which we can minister. Quiet giving and Christian love profit both the *Kingdom of God* and our lives in this world. When we are filled with joy and contentment, we are much more effective witnesses both with our mouths and with our lives. Will you begin to learn to give freely, building up treasures which do not perish,[27] or will you fall for the seduction of this world and ignore the sacrifice Jesus made for you at Calvary? He gave the ultimate gift and we should always be conscious of His giving when we are determining ours.[28]

ADDITIONAL SCRIPTURES

1. Luke 4:18, 14:21 & 18:22
2. Galatians 6:2 & 3
3. Isaiah 58:6 & 7
4. James 2:15 & 16
5. II Corinthians 9:6-9
6. Galatians 6:7
7. Matthew 6:3 & 4
8. II Timothy 3:1-9
9. Matthew 23:23, Luke 11:42 & Luke 18:12
10. I Timothy 6:5-12
11. Isaiah 55:8 & 9
12. II Corinthians 9:7

13. II Corinthians 9:6-15
14. John 21:21 & 22
15. Matthew 6:33
16. I John 4:1
17. Judges 17:6
18. I Timothy 6:15 & 16
19. Luke 10:7
20. II Corinthians 8:12
21. Hebrews 13:2
22. Philippians 4:19
23. II Corinthians 11:14
24. I John 4:1
25. Luke 6:38
26. Romans 12:1
27. Luke 12:33
28. John 3:16 & 17

STEP TWELVE

Discovering our calling was, for Linda and me, a time of change and of learning. The changes were many and the outward appearances of some of them were difficult to understand. As we said earlier, we had many possessions at the time we were saved. Linda had her high-paying job with it's accompanying BMW, I had a good job in the automobile business, and we owned a business on the side that was becoming very successful. In fact, to fit our budget, our income needed to be over $5,000 a month. We lived in a three-story condo with a pool and Jacuzzi right outside on our patio. The furnishings inside our home were opulent and expensive. As an example, our bed cost about $4,500. All of this may have been OK for someone else, but for us it represented things which caused us to decide that certain activities were unacceptable in terms of serving the Lord. We had to spend so much time taking care of our things that we were putting God second!

At the same time, we were earnestly seeking the Lord and His will for our lives. Obviously something had to give. Since we are writing this book, it wasn't our commitment to serve our Lord and Savior, Christ Jesus. As He removed all of the hindrances to

our service, the Lord also was blessing us with new
desires. Some of these were a hunger for His Word,
a constant desire to be in communication with Him
and to fellowship with others who had been locked in
bondages. The group we joined was "New Life Fellowship" and it provided some very necessary elements to cause us to grow in the Lord. The pastor,
John Rutherford, was willing to teach, counsel, encourage, admonish, exhort, and rebuke us as was
necessary. Even though some of this was uncomfortable at times, we knew John loved us and we were
willing to "do whatever it took," to find our place in
the Kingdom of God.

Eventually, it was time to step out in faith to
serve the Lord, and we began to pray. The first step
in our journey was to a place I dreaded. If I hadn't
been sure that the Lord wanted us to go there, I'd
never have considered it. The Lord sent us to
Wenatchee, Washington. The reason I didn't want to
go there, was that I had been involved in an outlaw
motorcyle club in that area. Some folks there would
like to end my life, if they could find me. Also the
police, no doubt, still had warrants for my arrest.
When the call became unmistakable, I simply said to
the Lord, "You know the ending before we begin; if
You are sending me, I'll go. I will trust my whole life
to You and I know that You will always be with me; I
know that no trouble can befall me that You aren't
capable of and willing to overcome or cause to be for
Your Glory."

When we arrived there, we both went to work and
waited to find out what the Lord had for us. Before

long, we were getting involved in the Christian community and finding a need for the same ministering which we had received in "New Life." We called John and told him what was going on and after we all prayed together, it was decided that we would plant a new fellowship right there. Through the power of His Spirit, God greatly blessed that fellowship and used us to start more in other areas also. The more we trusted the Lord, the more we found Him to be worthy of that trust. There are no limits to what God can do when we will serve Him. Through the years, He has taught, strengthened, caused to grow, and shown us much fruit in the work He has called us to do, and we are confident that He will be as trustworthy in the future as He has always been in the past.

Some of you are no doubt wondering what happened with my old enemies and with the Police; here is a short recap. We found that those who would have desired to get revenge were either in prison, dead or born again and serving the Lord. As for the police, somehow (we know how), all the criminal records of my past had disappeared. In fact, they gave me a key to the county jail visitation area so we could minister when needed. So much for fear and doubt!

We don't know what the future holds, but we do know that if the Lord wills it, the future will be better than anything we could have imagined or caused by our own work. One of the greatest blessings we have discovered is being able to trust the Lord in tough times. It is easy to trust Him when life is a

bowl of cherries, but when you are being bombarded
by the pits, trusting Him gives peace which overcomes all hardships and minor inconveniences. Though
it is not always easy, learning to lean on Him is the
most secure route for life that is available and He
will never let you down.

We could take pages and pages to give testimonies
about the miracle power of God in our lives and in
the lives of people He has ministered to through our
willingness to serve Him in whatever capacity He
chooses. As we progressed on our pilgrim pathway,
there were times when we became frustrated with,
or tired of dealing with people. A couple of times we
even tried to run away from the Lord; we discovered
that it is as the Bible says, impossible. Each time we
got weak, the Lord in His infinite mercy, loved us
back to His service. Don't misunderstand, we didn't
return to our sinful prior lives, we just tried to take
our family and hide from the world. We adopted
the attitude of "Us Four and No More." It
doesn't work.

Whatever the Lord calls you to do, your joy will be
in the calling and you will feel lower than a snail's
belly when you aren't working at it. Once we have
tasted the good things of the Lord, everything else is
colorless, tasteless, boring, and drudgery. We truly
can testify that the *Joy of the Lord* is our strength.
At no time have we ever found the Lord's work to be
anything other than exciting, colorful, uplifting, and
challenging. Experiencing the joy of seeing the solution to a problem or situation which seems insoluble
in our sight, is an experience which will never cease

to excite you and cause you to have even more trust in the Lord.

During our years in the ministry, people have tried to kill us, defame us, slander us, cheat us, steal from us, and many other things. What they didn't realize is that it was *The Living Lord* they were attacking. What I mean is that all of our substance, our lives, our reputation, our all, belongs to Him and we will spend it according to His will. If I don't own anything and don't possess anything of value to me except my eternal life with the Lord, what can anyone do to hurt me?

Let us encourage you to follow the Lord come what may; you'll never find anyone else who cares for you in truth. He died for you and me and will love us inspite of ourselves. Let us leave you with a thought about serving the Lord. In your life, have you ever found anything that didn't let you down, hurt you in the long run, betray you for a price, or prove to be less than you had anticipated? If you will answer that question honestly, you are still looking. Please take our advice, you won't find anyone who is trustworthy outside of *God's Eternal Kingdom*, so do as the Word of God says in Psalm 34:8 -

O taste and see that the Lord [our God] is good! Blessed (happy, fortunate, to be envied) is the man who trusts and takes refuge in Him.

You may also see I Peter 2:2 & 3.

May God bless you as you proceed with your "new life" in Christ Jesus. If you have completed this book

and still haven't made a decision for Christ, may the
Holy Spirit of God continue to convict you of your
sinful condition, and through your circumstances
bring you, like millions of others to a brokenhearted
confession and acceptance of Jesus as your Lord and
Savior that your joy may be full too!

STEP TWELVE
DISCOVER YOUR CALLING

**We have begun our search for the will of
God in our lives. How can we spend it to
benefit His Kingdom?   In our service to
the Master, it is our availability not our
ability that counts!**

This step will be a little different from the other
eleven you have just completed. We feel that this
step is of paramount importance to your future well-
being as a Christian, and, therefore, have taken the
liberty of changing the format. We think you will
find it beneficial and uplifting as well as stimulating
while you go through it. It is our prayer that this
step, as well as the other eleven, cause you to be
stimulated to go even deeper into God's Word to
answer questions that were raised. As you complete
step twelve, take an inventory of what changes have
been accomplished in your life by the *Living Word of
God.* If you find yourself slipping or having problems from time to time, go back to the appropriate
step or steps and reinforce your "New Life."

Discovering your calling will be both a help and a new challenge for you and we encourage you to step into it when you are certain of it. We don't, however, recommend that you get saved on Wednesday and on Thursday embark on a whole new career or decide that you are to enter a seminary and become a Doctor of Theology. Something like that may indeed be in your calling, but get to know your Savior and learn to recognize His voice before rushing into anything. Remember, when you were a newborn baby you didn't get up and run. Learn to walk first, and then you will be able to make a much more mature decision.

We do believe that every Christian has a calling and that there are a few titles you won't find in the job descriptions. Some of these titles are: Judge, Bible Writer, Unlocker of Divine Mysteries, Revealer of New Prophecy and Pew Pilot. The Lord has something for all of us who are His joint heirs to do, and it is up to us to prayerfully discover what that will be. We also believe that the route to finding your calling is expressed in the scripture that we are about to spell out for you. The process may seem obscure to you at first, but persevere and you will see what we mean.

Be sure, all the while, that you keep steps six, seven and eight fresh in your mind. This can be considered the tripod of your faith. What we mean is that if you had an expensive camera, you wouldn't put it on the ground or on a flimsy support, would you? No, you would put it on a strong and dependable tripod. Our tripod is made up of the following:

• Studying the Word of God consistently and daily,

• Developing a continuing scriptural prayer life, and

• Fellowshipping with your brothers and sisters in
  the Lord!

I can think of no stronger support for your most
valuable possession, your eternal life with the Almighty God, Jesus Christ our Lord and Savior, and
the Holy Spirit! AMEN!!

II Peter 1:2-11 & 19 -

> *(2) May grace (God's favor) and peace (which
> is perfect well being, all necessary good, all
> spiritual prosperity, and freedom from fears
> and agitating passions and moral conflicts)
> be multiplied to you in [the full, personal,
> precise, and correct] knowledge of God and of
> Jesus our Lord.*

> *(3) For His divine power has bestowed upon
> us all things that [are requisite and suited] to
> life and godliness, through the [full, personal]
> knowledge of Him Who called us by and to
> His own glory and excellence (virtue).*

> *(4) By means of these He has bestowed on us
> His precious and exceedingly great promises,
> so that through them you may escape [by
> flight] from the moral decay (rottenness and
> corruption) that is in the world because of
> covetousness (lust and greed), and become
> sharers (partakers) of the divine nature.*

> *(5) For this very reason, adding your diligence
> [to the divine promises], employ every effort in*

exercising your faith to develop virtue (excellence, resolution, Christian energy), and in [exercising] virtue [develop] knowledge (intelligence).

(6) And in [exercising] knowledge [develop] self-control, and in [exercising] self-control [develop] steadfastness (patience, endurance), and in [exercising] steadfastness [develop] godliness (piety).

(7) And in [exercising] godliness [develop] brotherly affection, and in [exercising] brotherly affection [develop] Christian love.

(8) For as these qualities are yours and increasingly abound in you, they will keep [you] from being idle or unfruitful unto the [full personal] knowledge of our Lord Jesus Christ (the Messiah, the Anointed One).

(9) For whoever lacks these qualities is blind, [spiritually] short-sighted, seeing only what is near to him, and has become oblivious [to the fact] that he was cleansed from his old sins.

(10) Because of this, brethren, be all the more solicitous and eager to make sure (to ratify, to strengthen, to make steadfast) your calling and election; for if you do this, you will never stumble or fall.

(11) Thus there will be richly and abundantly provided for your entry into the eternal kingdom of our Lord and Savior, Jesus Christ.

(19) And we have the prophetic word [made] firmer still. You will do well to pay close attention to it as to a lamp shining in a dismal (squalid and dark) place, until the day breaks through [the gloom] and the Morning Star rises (comes into being) in your hearts.

This may seem like an impossible task if we look at it in it's totality. What it will be is a lifelong journey which will take you on an adventure the likes of which you could never imagine. The way to approach it is the same way a friend of mine answers the question, "How do you eat an elephant? One bite at a time." The promises contained in this section of the Bible are awesome and are all for those of us who will persevere. Keep in mind though, your performance and ability will not be as important as the desire of your heart.

In verses 5 through 7 we see that we are to work and develop the attributes mentioned. Each is a little loftier than the one before and will carry rewards commensurate with it. It should be noted that the only man ever to live who could honestly say that He possessed all of these was Christ Jesus. However, this doesn't diminish the worthiness of the goal of attaining them. As you grow in these qualities you will find yourself more active in the *Body of Christ* (the church), more productive in your calling, and more at peace with the Lord. On the other side of it, we see that if we do not endeavor to develop these attributes, we will undoubtedly fall back into our old life with all of its pain and misery.

We are promised that if we steadfastly seek to grow and learn how to be more Christ-like, not only will our calling be sure, but we will never fall from our "new life" into the hog wallow we came from.[1] On top of everything else, we are promised that our entrance into Heaven will be marvelously and sumptuously provided for.[2] We should have as our goal, building treasures in Heaven,[3] and not being anxious about the state of our temporary existence in this squalid and dark world below.[4]

If you have just completed this book, let us congratulate you; most who begin it will never finish. Even something as life changing as the *Word of God* will be too much trouble for most, and some simply haven't suffered enough at the hands of Satan to come humbly before the throne of God. We can't imagine anyone who could finish this entire book and not have had a life-changing experience and we pray that during this journey through God's Word you have decided to join the family of God. If you haven't, rest assured that we will be praying daily that you will, in time, come to your senses.

The blessed hope we have in Christ Jesus is the only hope left in this lost and dying world.

As you go forward in your new freedom, keep this book and use it as a tool to keep your grasp on your "new life" firm. You may have noticed by now that this book is clearly for anyone who doesn't know the Lord Jesus as his personal Savior. The compulsion it is designed for is the sin nature which resides in all of us. The disease we are trying to combat is humanity. We don't at all agree with the humanists

who say that man is basically good with a tendency
to do bad once in a while. Anyone who has ever read
a history book knows that theory is a crock! We
believe that man is basically evil with an accidental
act of good slipping through once in a while. It is our
sincere desire that anyone who has discovered the
hopelessness of their life will come to the Cross and
meet Jesus, to discover His unfailing love and mercy.

To those of you who have believed already, let us
encourage you to continue on, learning to love and
learning to live life as God intends it to be lived by
His *Beloved Children.* Jesus, at the *Cross of Calvary*
defeated two of the three properties of sin; that is,
the power (the ability to force us to do Satan's will)
and the penalty ("The wages of sin is death," Romans
6:23). The only property of sin left is the presence of
sin on earth and our Lord is coming soon to deliver
us even from that into an eternity spent in fellowship with the Father.

Keep in mind that there are basically five positions we can be in as descendents of Adam:

1. Rebellion
2. Retribution
3. Repentance
4. Restoration
5. Rest.

Steps four and five can only be reached by step
three, there is no other way. If and when you find
yourself in an act of sin, reach God immediately in
prayers of repentance.[5] Don't let Satan convince you

of the lie that God won't forgive you. He is like the father in the parable of the lost son;[6] He is waiting for you to come home with open arms no matter how you have wasted your inheritance.

Most of all, let us exhort you to reach out to others who are hurting like you were. Help them to find what you have found! If this book has helped you find the Savior, or if you need additional help or information, please write or call us, we are interested in you!

Just Say Yes Ministries, Inc.
P.O. Box 2126
San Marcos, CA 92069
(619) 432-0557

ADDITIONAL SCRIPTURES

1. II Peter 2:22
2. Revelation 2:7, 11, & 17
3. Matthew 6:19-20 & John 14:1-3
4. Matthew 6:31-34
5. I John 1:8-9
6. Luke 15:11-32

EPILOGUE

About four years ago the Lord Jesus gave us a vision of an undertaking which is just about to become a reality. Not only were Linda and I convinced that the Lord had truly spoken to us, but He also confirmed our vision by showing our pastor, Greg Austin, what He had in store for us. Initially He only showed Linda and me a small portion of the vision, but as time progressed, He revealed more of it as we needed to know more. We don't have a precise time-table but we believe, without a doubt, He will cause all of the necessary doors to open and the wrong ones to close, so that His plan will be completed when He wills it.

There is a critical need for facilities which will provide not only a place for people who are coming out of destroyed lives, but also a place where they can be taught discipleship and how to survive in the world outside of the Church. The biggest problem we have seen in our work with street people and people with compulsive behavior disorders is that when they find their way to the Lord, they have very little chance to obtain ongoing help. Our dear friends who run rescue missions are doing all they can, but they need the next step. Once a person is "dried out and straight" where will they go and where will they be welcomed? In our modern Churches with their expensive buildings and more expensive programs? Sadly, this will not happen. As much as some of the membership will be willing to help, the majority will not welcome the unlovely and those with little or no social grace. When an individual or family has had their life destroyed by the excesses of sin, they need a "city of refuge" where they can be nurtured and instructed while the Lord is restoring their lives.

The following outline is a basic sketch of our vision:

JUST SAY YES RANCH
OBJECTIVES

I. To provide a facility for the restoration of the lives of families and individuals who have been delivered from the excesses of a sin-filled life.

   A. To provide a Christian facility to help those families and individuals learn to survive both in the Church and in the world outside of the Church

      1. Full range community outreach center for re-education.

      2. Job search assistance.

      3. Health care assistance.

   B. To provide a counselling and support service for the families of individuals who are having problems with chemical addiction or abuse.

1. Education directed towards obtaining deliverance and healing for the entire family of the addicted person.

2. Financial, spiritual, and intrafamily relationship counselling for the addict's family.

3. Financial, spiritual, medical, and nutritional aid for the addict's family.

C. To provide guidance and training to cause lifestyle changes which are necessary in overcoming abuse and addiction.

1. Necessary re-education for families to facilitate growth in their new life in Christ Jesus.

2. Training to alter behavior patterns of the family which cause addictive responses.

3. Guidance in locating new friends and relationships which will promote growth in their new lives.

4. Basic job training to facilitate re-entry into mainstream life, as necessary.

II. To provide community support services along with the counselling and support facility.

A. Provide shelter for families and individuals with chemical abuse or addiction problems (including alcohol).

1. Institute Christian primary and secondary education programs as the need arises.

2. Institute on-site discipleship training program.

3. Provide Christian-oriented recreation and fellowship opportunities.

B. To provide temporary shelter for individuals and families who otherwise would have none.

    1. To provide meals as needed.

    2. To provide food boxes to families in need.

    3. Establish a clothes closet program.

At this time we have 826 acres on which to build the pilot project. Our needs are many and we would welcome any help the Lord would have you offer.

Our facility will be a working ranch which will be as self supporting as possible. The goal of the ranch is to enable those who come to us needing help to be able to return to productive lives, serving the Lord. We will not, however, be a detoxification or treatment center and will, therefore, only accept families and individuals who have been sober and straight for a predetermined length of time.

We would like to stress the concept of a "working" ranch. No one will be coming to us to lay around and continue dwelling in their past problems. We feel there are already too many "free rides" in our society. Again, if you are touched in your spirit by our vision please contact us for further details and information.

Linda and I realize that only a few are called to work directly with this type of people and, therefore, we are looking for those who are called to support such works with their prayers, and whatever else the Lord directs them to give. Money is always an issue, but we wish to assure everyone that money is not our biggest need. Please prayerfully support us and respond as the Lord directs.

Order Additional Copies of

JUST SAY YES
Today!

Trade paperback suggested donation $8.00

When you order your book, any gift over and above the $8.00 suggested donation will be used to distribute books to those who couldn't otherwise afford one. Your generosity will be appreciated.

Name_____Phone_____

Address_____

City_____State_____Zip_____

I would like _____ copies   Total enclosed $_____

Send this order form to:

Just Say Yes Ministries, Inc.
P.O. Box 2126
San Marcos, CA 92069